Mostly Mama

FOR ALL THE HEROS IN THE WORLD
BUT
MOSTLY WEE

BECAUSE IN MY books
YOU'RE SPECIAL !!

Lewis Meyer

By the same author:

PREPOSTEROUS PAPA

SECOND WIFE

THE CUSTOMER IS ALWAYS

OFF THE SAUCE

Mostly Mama

by Lewis Meyer

Doubleday & Company, Inc., Garden City, New York, 1971

Library of Congress Catalog Card Number 72–144281
Copyright © 1971 by Lewis Meyer
All Rights Reserved
Printed in the United States of America

To Natasha

Contents

	Introduction	9
1.	It Used to Be Called Asylum Avenue	11
2.	Tight Shoe Night	43
3.	Mama Herself	77
4.	"I've Got a Feelin' You're Foolin'"	97
5.	Send Me a Postcard When You Reach the Top	127
6.	Sma Faw	143
7.	"My Wrists Are Weak"	173
8.	Onward, Pilgrim Soldiers	199

Introduction

Apologize to Mama for writing *Preposterous Papa* first? No need to. It was she who made the rules and Rule Number One said that Papa was head of the house. In our family, Papa was spoken to first, served first, minded first. Mama saw to it that nobody dared do it any other way.

This book is mostly about Mama. It is the story of my mother's life as I remember it. Unlike many biographies, there is no attempt at chronology. Memories (at least my own) do not come and go in any logical time sequence. They *are*. These incidents which show Mama for what she was are told as I remember them, unchronologically.

One thing for sure: Mama was preposterous in her own right . . . not merely because she lived with a bigger-than-life man like Max Meyer.

The book is true. These things happened. I have changed only a place name or two and the names of living people. Sapulpa, Oklahoma, is real. (Imagine trying to invent a name to top Sapulpa!) Oak Street is still there—but both the house on Oak Street and the ranch house no longer exist as they were.

I grew up in Oklahoma when the state and most of the people in it were young. I like remembering it that way and am not ashamed to admit that I am more at home in the world of yesterday than I am in the world of today. Not wanting to let go of the past is a kind of compliment to those who brought us up. I hope my own children will feel the same way.

1. It Used to Be Called Asylum Avenue

I was six years old the first time I heard Papa refer to my "screwin'-around" Uncle Sam. Papa and Mama were talking privately on the platform outside the Pullman car a couple of minutes before the train left for Texas. My sisters were already in the stateroom with our little brother, Manny. I ran up and down the narrow, carpeted aisle, restraining my curiosity to peek inside the heavy, green drapes that concealed the upper and lower berths, then wandered onto the vestibule where I stood quietly and listened in on Papa's last-minute instructions.

"Don't take no for an answer," he said emphatically. "Tell Ed that you have to have five thousand dollars and not a penny less." He took her hand, gripped it, and pumped it up and down for emphasis. "For God's sake, don't tell him it's for land. Tell Ed we owe money in the store and if he doesn't give you five thousand dollars right now we'll go bankrupt."

"Bankrupt," Mama repeated absently. She was vaguely

aware that Max was using a subtle form of blackmail to get his money. No Levy, not even a Levy in-law, had ever taken bankruptcy.

"Got to have it, Annie. One hundred and sixty acres right next to the ranch. If I don't buy it somebody else will and then it'll be too late. It's for the kids. They'll have land when they grow up and land is the best insurance."

Mama looked toward the engine. She always got nervous just before the train started. "Ed says—"

"I know what Ed says. Ed's afraid of land, Ed's afraid of spending money, Ed's afraid of everything. Look at that beat-up Chevrolet he drives. And those threadbare suits. He's in charge of all the Levy money and he acts like a pauper. Tell Ed you're only asking for what's rightfully yours."

"He gets mad when I say that."

"If you want to wait for the Levys to give you your share of your father's estate you'll wait forever. Ed may get mad but he doesn't stay mad."

"Here comes the conductor," Mama said, edging toward the stool under the high first step.

Papa was talking fast now, trying to get everything in. "Keep the kids away from Sam. He's always screwin' around." He lowered his voice. "Make them use Mabel's bathroom. Every time you take the kids to Texas I worry they'll catch something."

"Sam's all right," Mama protested. "He's high-spirited."

"High-spirited, hell," I heard Papa say. "He's just weak. But not too weak to screw anything that'll hold still. If they have to use his bathroom make them put paper on the seat."

The conductor sauntered up, took his gold grandfather watch from his vest pocket, pressed the spring that opened its case, watched the second hand touch ten markers, then said gently to Mama, "All aboard, Mrs. Meyer."

I began to get agitated because Mama still hadn't got onto the train even though the conductor had warned her. What if the train pulled out before she could get on it, with the four of us children marooned in that stateroom like abandoned orphans?

"Hurry up, Mama!" I yelled in a shrill voice that made both Mama and Papa jump. They were unaware of my being just above them. "Hurry!"

Mama quickly kissed Papa on the cheek and turned toward the train but he pulled her back to him and kissed her on the mouth for what seemed a long time and then he lifted her right up to the second step of the Pullman car. The train took its first tentative move as Papa said to the conductor (the way he always did), "Take good care of my little family, Bert."

I remember feeling the cinders against my cheek and smelling the smoke from the engine and seeing Papa standing there smiling and waving at us as the conductor neatly grabbed the little stool, swung onto the coach and shut the gate above the steps. Then the conductor stepped aside and let Mama lift me up so we could both lean over the gate and wave at Papa.

"Be a good boy!" he shouted at me. He always said, "Be a good boy" every time we went anyplace. And then he'd add, "And mind your mama." I was waiting for him to say that last part as he always did but this time he cupped his hands to his mouth and yelled instead, "Don't take no for an answer, Annie darling . . . And not one penny less than . . ." He had to scream the last word but he made it. *"Five!"*

Texas was another world from Oklahoma. The air had a different smell to it and the natives talked more Southern than they did at home. Everything moved slower. People complained about how hot the weather was for June but most of the men wore suits and hardly any children got to go barefoot.

Mama, little Manny and I stayed in the Main House while my sisters, Bea and Pearl, stayed with their girl cousins across the street. Everywhere I looked I'd see an aunt or uncle or cousin. They all lived together in the Levy compound which meandered up and down Levy Avenue on both sides of the street, a strange and inbred fixture of Taro, Texas. They had settled here more than fifty years ago, married here, and in many instances intermarried here.

Next to the Main House was a three-story-plus residence (that would have twinned its neighbor but for the lack of a steeple) belonging to Aunt Mamie and Cousin Iz. Cousin Iz was supposed to be very rich from oil and owned, among other things, the Palace Confectionery downtown. Cousin Iz had never married and Mama would sigh as she said, "Izzy has devoted his life to his mother." His mother was Aunt Mamie, a frail woman who walked with a cane, quoted Shakespeare, and who always seemed to be dressed for a party in her long-sleeved, high-necked black taffeta dresses. Next door to Cousin Iz and Aunt Mamie was Uncle Ed's house, a modest one-story bungalow. Uncle Ed had married Aunt Mamie's daughter, Nellie, and since they were first cousins their children were double Levys. Farther along in the same block were Aunt Sarah and Uncle Harry and then, on a corner, Cousin Tillie and Cousin Francis.

Directly across the street from the Main House were Aunt Josie and her three daughters, Marilyn, Maxine and Midge.

You could count four houses to the left of Aunt Josie and
five houses to the right and still get more Levys. There were
dozens of them . . . Helen and Don (also first cousins) and
Aunt Becky who lived with her daughter Ethelene, and
Cousin Walter and his wife, Myrtle, and old Uncle Ike. . . .
You could spot a Levy from the curly orange hair, the bump
on the bridge of the aquiline nose, the skinny frame, the
high cheekbones, and always the thick glasses over the green-
hazel eyes. Alas, when Levy married Levy myopia married
myopia and there was no dominant eye gene to prevail.

Papa, who despised everything about Taro, never lost a
chance to remind people that Levy Avenue was originally
called Asylum Avenue after the state institution at the far
end of it. "It's crazier as Levy Avenue than it was before,"
he liked to add. He also took pains to point out that Mama,
with her lustrous black hair, large brown eyes, perfect vision
and straight nose didn't look like one of "them." He said,
"Old Philip Levy started a gravy train and his descendants
have been eating off it ever since." The Levys hadn't taken
too kindly to Papa and he was openly contemptuous of their
frailties. "They live so close together they don't know how to
mind their own business." According to Papa, if Cousin Francis
did something unmentionable at his end of the avenue Cousin
Helen whiffed it at the opposite end.

Mama loved it all. In a way, this was still her home. She
was born in the Main House and had lived very happily in
and out of all the houses on this street until she married
"that Arkansas interloper" (her father's expression), who
"married out of his class." Her deepest roots were in these
few blocks and they were still a part of her. It had taken
equal amounts of love and courage for her to give up the
double-cream life she had lived as a girl, which included

her father's own opera house above his store and annual Levy vacation trips to faraway places, for the raw and dusty life of Sapulpa, Oklahoma. She tried not to think too much about Taro when she was away from it, but whenever she returned for a visit she couldn't help thinking that she and Max and the children could be living comfortably (off the gravy train) in a house with a steeple on Levy Avenue if Max hadn't pulled that darned-fool stunt with the store safe. He learned the combination from watching Sam and Ed and her father open it and then, just to devil them, pretended he was a part-time safecracker and opened it himself. There had been other provocations but the safe was the proximate cause of their departure. As we grew up, Mama sometimes bragged about Papa's "pioneering spirit." When she did so, Papa would laugh and say, "Pioneering spirit, hell! I pioneered to Indian Territory because Annie's father kicked me out of Texas!" It was true. "Oklahoma's the land of opportunity, Max," his father-in-law had said. "Pick yourself a town and I'll build a store there for you and Annie." And so they were banished from the land of milk, honey and gravy trains.

Mama spent every minute of the first two days visiting her kin. She let my sisters play with their girl cousins over at Aunt Josie's but she dragged Manny and me from one Levy house to the other repeating a pattern:

"*Aunt Becky!*"

"*Annie Levy! . . . You look thin. . . . Come in and bring those two fine Levy boys.*"

"*They're Meyers, Aunt Becky. I'm a Meyer now . . . remember?*"

"*Humpf. You left him once. . . . They're Levys. They both have the Levy squint. Teena's been bakin' cookies all mawnin'.*"

Teeeeena! Get those cookies on a big plate and bring it in the parlor. Annie's home!"

Annie belonged to them. They loved her. Their voices all said: *So you married for love and what did you get? Four children and a hard life with a man who never even heard of Shakespeare! Come and let us hug you, child. Let us give you enough loving to last you a long time after you're back in that godforsaken place again.* There were cookies and kisses and tears and laughter from Sarah and Harry and Tillie and Josie and Iz and old Aunt Mamie and Becky and Ethelene and . . . *all* of them. Except maybe Ed. Ed knew what Mama had come after and Ed was in hiding. He hid because he loved Mama the most and he knew that once she pinned him down he'd weaken as he always did and give her the money Max had sent her after.

My old-maid aunt and two old-maid uncles lived in the Main House. Uncle Sam had a bedroom and bath on the first floor. Aunt Mabel shared with us the six rooms and two bathrooms she had accumulated on the second, and Uncle Julius lived in the two small rooms and one small bath that was the third floor.

Once each visit, if we were lucky, Mama would coax Uncle Julius into letting us invade his apartment so we could climb the rickety staircase to the tower above his room. Even though the tower was cobwebby and dark one could still make out the roof going to a point for its steepled crown. On my first visit there I begged for permission to open the small, heavily paned window, climb through it, and stroll around the narrow widow's walk, but Uncle Julius disappointed me by revealing that the window was unopenable and that the walk was merely nailed-on, fake outside trimming—gingerbread, he called it.

Grandpa Philip Levy had built this Main House for Grandma Lena a long time ago and here they had brought up their seven children. Now, both my grandmother and grandfather were dead and only Mabel, Sam and Julius rattled around in it.

My memories of the Main House always begin with colors because the downstairs entry hall, parlor and dining room had windows with colored glass panes. Some of these panes were of opaque white but most were rose, purple, green, blue and yellow. When the sun shone through them the rugs and floors had patches of beautiful colors. Children's hands could be almost any color you wished simply by moving them a few inches in any direction. All windows facing Levy Avenue had wooden shutters, each with dozens of tiny louvers. What fun it was to place one's fingers on the shutters' spines and push them up and down to make the slats open and close!

The entryway was a room in itself but there were no chairs or furniture except a hall tree for coats and umbrellas. There were no rugs on its dark, polished hardwood floor and very little light other than that which came in through the colored panes of a purely decorative, protruding bay window. What made the entryway impressive was the lack of a first-floor ceiling in order for it to accommodate a truly marvelous staircase that began with four extra-wide steps, paused briefly for a platform landing, proceeded up eight steps to another landing, then made an abrupt right turn and climbed six more. The banisters were about as large as a boy's arms, were round and made of reddish-brown wood. The banister at each landing had an ornamental round cherrywood ball bigger than my head, strategically placed to discourage youngsters like me from taking a short-cut slide instead of the steps. There were four of these highly polished balls, one on the ground floor, one on that spectacular first landing, one where the stairs turned right and one at the very top. A child can lose track of time while running his hand around smooth round ornaments like those cherrywood balls and the banisters they graced.

Under the staircase was a strange, slant-roofed nook which Mama called the fruit closet (because that's what her own mother had used it for). The fruit closet was always locked and therefore off-bounds to prying nieces and nephews. Off-bounds only to nephews was the painfully bright-green carpeted parlor which opened off the entry and continued along the front of the house.

On the questionable theory that girls are less destructive than boys my sisters and girl cousins were permitted the use of the parlor while my little brother and I were forbidden to step a foot inside it. My sister Bea was allowed to practice her piano there on what Aunt Mabel called "the big baby grand" and the other girls were free to play records on the phonograph. While the piano bored me, the phonograph was such a wondrous thing I harbored a reservoir of six-year-old bitterness at being forbidden to place my ear at its speaker. I was constantly begging my sisters to play certain records over and over while I sat on the polished floor of the adjoining entry hall and listened. My favorite was a kind of recitation to a musical background entitled "Cohen Owes Me Ninety-Seven Dollars." In it, a father who is on his deathbed calls in his children to give them his last instructions which begin, "Cohen owes me ninety-seven dollars. . . . It's up to you to see that Cohen pays. . . ." Other records I kept re-

19

questing were "The Stars and Stripes Forever," "Humoresque," "The Japanese Sandman" and Fanny Brice's "Second Hand Rose."

There was a back staircase which went straight up—zoom! —eighteen steps with no landings or cherrywood balloons. This staircase was in the back part of the house and to reach it one had to walk through the dining room, then through an odd-shaped room no one ever used, which had green velvet furniture and a green-and-white striped satin love seat, and then, finally, through a kind of catchall utility room. It was always dark under the back staircase, and the single light fixture on the wall was much too small. In the deepest shadows under the stairs was the icebox. The iceman always had to pause for a moment after coming in from the bright sunlight to get his bearings before he could deposit his block of ice in the chest.

A few steps away was Emma's enormous kitchen kingdom with its huge wood stove, its built-in cupboards, its counters, tubs, basins, work tables, shelves of dishes and tin-lined kitchen sink. Emma must have been a very young girl when she came to work for my grandparents (she still referred to them as Miz Lena and Mistuh Philip) because she was still frying chicken, whipping potatoes and making flaky-crusted green apple pies when I was in college. Surely Emma's ghost is in that kitchen today, baking panfuls of light-as-a-feather hot biscuits, slathering them with her own churned butter, and serving them with side dishes of honey from the Levys' own beehives at the far end of the back yard. (The beehives were off-bounds for nieces, nephews, uncles, aunts and cousins. Only Emma's husband, Varney, knew how to handle the bees.)

I wish my own children could have met Varney before

he died. Varney was one part Johnny Appleseed, one part Jack of the Beanstalk, and one part God the way he made things grow. Aside from the bees, and the kindling box in Emma's kitchen, and the errands he ran for Uncle Sam (Varney knew the most responsible bootleggers), it would take at least three ghosts to do his yardwork alone. He never got tired. If he was not cutting grass or watering, he was on his hands and knees trimming along walks or weeding and mulching the two great flower circles on either side of the walk from the street to the front porch. One circle had at least three dozen giant rose bushes, many of them planted by Grandma Lena years before. The other circle was thick with canna lilies which had leathery green leaves with sticky points and bright orange blossoms.

Around the entire Levy property was a chest-high, black iron fence with hundreds of dividers, every sixth one crowned with a black wrought-iron Star of David. There would be less insecurity in the world if more children had access to fences like that one. The tactile sensation of pride and power that came from running one's fingers along its prongs was surpassed only by the joy of compressing the latch on the iron gate and swinging on it until someone in authority made you stop.

Uncle Sam seemed to understand how I felt about the fence and gate because he would go there with me after supper and even push me to and fro on the gate. But Aunt Mabel and Uncle Julius preferred to give me dimes and urge me to "Run off and play someplace" or "Why don't you sit on the swing on the side porch and wave at Aunt Mamie?" In the twenties grownups were more delicate in their communications with nephews. They may have thought Get Lost, but they didn't come right out and say it. Mama spent a good deal of time explaining to me that Mabel and Julius didn't

21

dislike me; they just weren't used to having children around. They really loved me (she said) and they "didn't mean any harm." I didn't argue. I enjoyed swinging on the porch and waving at old Aunt Mamie (who never waved back) and, besides, I was making at least fifty cents a day in bribes.

In between swinging, waving, going up and down staircases, getting handouts from Emma in the kitchen and pestering Varney around the yard I got some very definite impressions of my aunt and uncles, impressions which I have somehow been unable to lose or forget, though there have been times when I wish I could.

It is unfair to call any woman a born old maid but Aunt Mabel really and truly was one. She wouldn't have left the second floor of the Main House for the best catch in the world. She lived contentedly in a sea of untidiness so choppy it appalled her six-year-old visitor.

"Mama," I whispered, "why is Aunt Mabel so messy?"

Mama, who itched to put a semblance of order into that overflowing pushcart of a second floor, wisely kept her hands off Mabel's chaos. "At home we pick things up and put them away," Mama explained. "But when we come to Taro we are guests and should not criticize. Your Aunt Mabel is a . . . a collector."

Aunt Mabel was a collector, all right, and because she was never positive that a new addition to her collection was there for keeps she put it where she could see it in the meantime. There were piles of linens, piles of materials, piles of blouses, open wardrobes stuffed with dresses of every mode and vintage, and two rooms of shoes, most of them in the original boxes.

The long hall that hinged the rooms was wide enough to

accommodate a series of cedar chests on both sides of it. These chests (no one ever referred to them as hope chests because there plainly was no hope for Mabel) were packed with items which evidently had been seasoned for a sufficient period of time to become permanent parts of her collection. One contained sheets and cases of every kind and description, bath towels, guest towels and costly spreads; another was filled with pieces of cloth, hundreds of dress lengths, drape yardage and upholstery materials; another with lingerie, all unworn; and still another packed with blankets, quilts and comforters, all new, many with price tags still attached.

Mama wandered among the merchandise, spotting items which no longer interested her sister. She began mentally to pack some of the empty boxes Varney was accumulating for her, even before Mabel had been asked to concede a stitch. Uncle Sam had already yielded four suits, Uncle Julius two, and Mama figured that she might get at least one from Uncle Ed who wore things until they disintegrated. In her own way, Mama was as hopeless a collector as Aunt Mabel but Mama's acquisitions went straight to the Salvation Army where they were immediately disposed of. When she got home she would insist that Major Miller take the best of the Sam suits for himself. Luckily, Mrs. Major Miller was Mabel's size.

Papa often said that Major and Mrs. Miller held special prayer services at the Salvation Army Hut during Mama's Taro "hunting expeditions" to ensure a successful "kill." Surely the local corps sang a couple of extra hosannas whenever Mama returned home with her windfall of Levy rummage. Mama felt that she helped both ends. She opened up badly needed storage room for her brothers and sister while giving the Sapulpa Salvation Army a new lease on life.

Mabel sensed Mama's predatory inventorying and cautioned, petulantly, "Now, Annie, don't go toting things away until you let me see what you're taking. Some of these clothes are just on approval. I haven't bought them yet."

Nothing was officially "bought" by Aunt Mabel until it was used. She paid her bills promptly but it was not unusual for her to send back dresses or hats or sets of towels or pairs of shoes two full years after she had purchased them. "On approval" was her nice way of putting it. "Gall" was a nice way of putting what the merchants thought of Mabel's antics. If a store tried to resist her return she made life miserable for the clerk, department head or store manager who refused it, the mailman who brought it back, and the business office that denied her a credit. Indeed, she had her own bookkeeping system in which she gave herself credits even though the stores refused to do so. She never let them forget that her brother Julius was a lawyer and a legislator and that his roommate at the University of Texas Law School was the present Governor of Texas. Ultimately she won her point simply because the storekeepers were too exhausted to continue the fight.

We arrived at a touchy time because Mabel had just received a strong letter from Neiman-Marcus requesting her in very firm phrases to take her business elsewhere. Since Neiman's was her principal source of supply she was understandably upset. She kept roaming from room to room and cedar chest to cedar chest, pointing to all kinds of merchandise she had paid for and enumerating the thousands of dollars she had spent with Neiman-Marcus. "What thanks do I get for my devoted patronage? A nasty letter I could sue them for if I wasn't such a lady!"

It was comforting having Mama there to complain to.

Mabel didn't like to discuss things with the help, who were all vaguely related to Emma and who wandered lonely as clouds amidst the piles and stacks and boxes. Most of these helpers just floated in and out, afraid to touch anything except maybe to hang up an occasional robe, make an occasional bed or mop an occasional marble-top washstand.

Mabel considered Mama an ally and figured that since Mama was a Levy her honor had been offended, too. "We're going straight to Stanley Marcus," Aunt Mabel whined. "We're going straight to his private office and make him read this insulting letter." All Mama could do was nod sympathetically. "He's kind of in the family, y'know," Mabel continued. "Yes. Stanley Marcus's sister married a Rosenfelt, whose mother was a Levy by marriage. Or maybe it was his niece. Anyway, he's got to take our side in this fuss because he's one *of* us!"

Even as Mabel was sniffling her complaints she was planning a gigantic counteroffensive. She moved from pile to pile, lifting a nightgown here, a camisole there, a corselette, a shirtwaist dress, a hairbrush, a dresser scarf and earmarking them for return.

"We'll go to Dallas tomorrow, Annie. Just you and I. I'll pay for everything."

Mama nodded uncomfortably. She knew that the toughened Oklahoma sister would end up doing the dirty work. Every time Mama returned to Taro for a visit she was resigned to spending at least one dreadful day in Dallas where she took sacks or boxes of old merchandise to the proper counters, said quickly, "Please credit Miss Mabel Levy, Levy Avenue, Taro, Texas," and ran away just as the salespeople began their screaming hysterics.

Mabel always bought Mama a nice present for her trouble,

adding, "If you decide you don't like it when you get home just send it back and make them give you a credit."

But Mama, whose husband ran a store of his own, didn't like to play the returning game. She'd rather give something to that nice Marian Miller at the Salvation Army than return it to Stanley Marcus, even if he was a member of the family.

My Uncle Julius was a good man who smelled of bad cigars. He was extremely short, five foot two at the most, but he never seemed to have a complex about it. Perhaps his blaring voice was his own way of compensating. He was a living, breathing, public-address system. He would call to you and the sound of his voice would bounce against your cranium like a tennis ball, operate on your head like a buzz saw, clean the wax out of your ears. Whatever hackles are, one word from Uncle Julius and every hackle in the room jumped to attention.

He was pleasant whenever he greeted his nephews and nieces and was always good for a handout, but we didn't see much of him. He stayed to himself in his third-floor apartment with the door closed against us, smoking one stinking cigar after the other. I wondered a lot about what else he did when he was alone. I imagined his spending hours peering up and down Levy Avenue with powerful binoculars (how silly that was! Who in his right mind would want to spy on Aunt Mamie or Ethelene or Cousin Francis?), or writing letters to some of the famous people he knew, or listening to his crystal set radio, or maybe playing solitaire. I finally asked Aunt Mabel what he did up there and it was a terrible shock to learn from her that he read books. From my occasional peaks I had observed that his walls were solidly lined with books but I didn't dream that he sat down and read them. I remember feeling very sorry for him for having to spend his time that way.

Uncle Julius was evidently a good lawyer and a good mixer. He knew just about all the important people in Texas. He was constantly referring to his friend Sam, and I figured he meant Uncle Sam until I learned later on that it was Sam Rayburn. Aunt Mabel wasn't making it up about her brother being the roommate of the Governor of Texas when they were in law school. But she didn't add that Uncle Julius detested the Governor for christening him PeeWee. The name somehow stuck and many politicians (who didn't know better) still called him PeeWee Levy. Uncle Julius had served a term in the Texas legislature but he refused to run for re-election, preferring instead to be the Taro City Attorney, a post he would be elected and re-elected to for almost fifty years. He was the big wheel in the county Democratic machine and, at the time of our visit, was massing an all-out, PeeWee-David-against-Goliath attack on the Governor in the forthcoming primary.

Whenever people asked Mama why her brother Julius never married she'd say it was none of their business. There were plenty of theories about it, however, and with just a normal amount of circulating I learned several of them. Aunt Becky insisted that so long as Mabel didn't marry, Julius wouldn't, either. This didn't make a lot of sense because Mama told me that Aunt Mabel was older than Uncle Julius and was capable of taking care of herself. Besides, Uncle Ed was just two houses away and everyone knew that Ed worried over all the Levys.

My sisters, who were more curious about bachelors than I was, made me promise that I'd ask Varney about Uncle Julius. If I refused I knew they wouldn't play records for

me any more so I asked Emma to make some lemonade for
Varney and me and I took our glasses out to the back yard
where Varney was mowing the grass. While we sat on the
ground and drank our lemonade I asked him the question,
pretending to be very spur-of-the-moment about it and acting
as though I really didn't care.

Varney paused for a moment, then pointed at the two-
story white house whose back yard joined ours, just past
the Levy beehives. "Over yonder's where Miss Alice lives,"
he said. "Ev'body thought Mr. Julius would marry Miss Alice.
They been sweethearts since they was in the first grade.
But *her* people"—he pointed at the white house again—"are
Baptists and the Levys are Jews and I think they flat wouldn't
let her marry him 'cause of that." Varney took a gulp from
his glass of lemonade. "Mr. Julius takes Miss Alice to the
Texas State Fair ever' September and to the Rotary Sweet-
heart Banquet and things like that, and I guess they still
love each other, but they won't neither one of 'em marry
nobody now." He finished his lemonade. "Leastwise, not while
Miss Alice's mommy and daddy are alive."

Emma was to the point on Uncle Julius's celibacy. "Mr.
Julius won't never get married because he's too short." It
was a simple statement of fact which needed no embellish-
ment. "Miss Alice is head and shoulders taller than he is and
that's the whole reason."

But if Uncle Julius was unhappy because of his height or
his single state or the fact that he spent most of his time
with the door closed reading books and smoking cigars (my
own theory, in retrospect, is that a woman would have to be
desperate to marry a man who needed fumigating), he
never let on to the rest of us. He was always loud and
cheerful, loud and generous, *loud*. His voice assaulted our

eardrums and chased us up and down staircases. Uncle Julius put out more noise per square inch than a World War One howitzer. His voice bothered me then. Little did I dream how much it would continue to annoy, plague and mortify me in the years ahead.

As objectionable as his smelly cigars and his vocal excesses was Uncle Julius's refusal to call me by my rightful name. Or even by my rightful *two* names. It was the Texas custom to address a child by his or her full name. My cousins weren't just Marilyn or Maxine or Alfred or Philip. They were Marilyn Rose, Maxine Elizabeth, Alfred Ross or Philip Leon.

My first name happens to be Harry and I have always been ashamed of it. I lie on all questionnaires that demand "Name in Full" and have gone through life contentedly using only my middle name. (My own children will learn that their father is a Harry when they read these words.) But all the Levys except Uncle Julius called me Harry Lewis. They Texified Harry in such a way that it became three syllables instead of two and sounded like Hay-uh-ree Lewis. For a reason I have never understood, Uncle Julius insisted on calling me Lully.

I hate Harry, but I loathe Lully. There is nothing intrinsically wrong with the word Lully. It's just not for me. Uncle Julius insisted on Lullying me almost beyond endurance. My Lully complex was rooted in resentment when I was no more than four years old and eating a frap pay (it was two words at Cousin Izzy's Palace Confectionery), and Uncle Julius stuck his head inside the door and yelled at me in front of all my cousins, "Hurry up, Lully baby. We want to go home." Maybe everyone wasn't convulsed. Maybe I was just an oversensitive four and thought they were. But that frap pay had a Lully flavor to it and I've never been able to order another from that day to this.

Whenever Uncle Julius would take Mama and her children to Dallas for the day I dreaded getting into an elevator with him, particularly at Neiman-Marcus. Uncle Julius, who was invariably pinned into a corner in the rear of the car, would bellow from his low position, "Where *are* you, Lully?" People would shift in the crowded car, glancing down nervously to see if a dog named Lully was under their feet. I can tell you it wasn't easy.

Once, when I was ten or eleven years old, I told Uncle Julius I had to go to the toilet and he took me to the men's room in the Baker Hotel. It cost a nickel then and I worked the door myself. But I was not prepared for Uncle Julius charging through the swinging doors, staring at the long row of pay booths and screaming, "LULLY? Which one are you IN, Lully? Don't close the door when you come out and I'll give you the nickel we SAVE!"

As the years fly by I forget most of the things that happen to me, but I can enumerate one-two-three each and every time that I've been Lullied by Uncle Julius, whose voice, like cheese, grew stronger with age. In Peacock Alley at the Waldorf, from one end of a crowded subway car to the other, in my cap and gown walking in a solemn procession at Dartmouth College ("THERE he is! THERE'S our LULLY!"), and at the speakers' table of the Texas-Oklahoma Bar banquet I've cringed at Uncle Julius's affectionate salute.

When I was still a little boy I put my head in Mama's lap and whimpered, "If he doesn't stop calling me that name I'm going to call him PeeWee."

"Don't you dare!" Mama warned. She knew I was distressed because I didn't cry easily. "That would be cruel." She

sat me in a chair and wiped my eyes with her perfumy-smell-
ing handkerchief and said almost in a whisper, "Uncle Julius
doesn't mean to tease you. He doesn't like teasing because he's
been teased all his life for being so short. He calls you Lully
because he loves you. I'll tell Mabel and Sam and the others
to call you by your real name and if you're sweet to Uncle
Julius I promise that no one else will ever say that word you
don't like."

"For the rest of my life?"

"For the rest of your life."

"Harry, either—outside of Taro?"

"Harry, either. Cross my heart."

When Mama crossed her heart you could depend on it.
Both Harry and Lully ceased to exist except as parts of my
secret Texas life.

"Keep the kids away from Sam," Papa admonished, but
Mama must have forgotten what he said. Since Uncle Sam
was, hands down, my most exciting relative, I was glad that
Mama didn't try to keep me away from him. I gravitated to
him every chance I got and he always seemed pleased to
have me around.

At nine-twenty each morning I stationed myself on the
bottom step of the back staircase. Precisely at nine-thirty
Uncle Sam's alarm went off with such a wild clanging that I
jumped, even though I had been waiting for it. In his tightly
shuttered bedroom Sam let the alarm ring for a few seconds,
then groped for it and shut it off. While the echo was still
climbing the walls he opened his eyes wide and screamed,
"Emma . . . I *say:* Em-MUH!"

Emma was waiting, too. His tray was ready on the corner
of the kitchen counter where she could grab it and run at

31

the given signal. The tray held two heavy cut-glass tumblers, one filled with ice water, the other containing three ounces of Old Crow bourbon whiskey. It hadn't varied in twenty years. The same glasses (from Grandma Lena's best set), the ice water, the brand of whiskey, the three ounces.

While his pitiful cry was still reverberating in the dining room, in the funny shaped room with the green velvet furniture, through the utility room and into the kitchen, Emma had already dashed by me and was opening his bedroom door. "Mawnin', Mistuh Sam," she always said as she deposited the tray on the bedside table nearest him. ("Mistuh Sam never wakes up on the same side twicet in a row!") Then she turned and headed back for the kitchen.

"Thank you, Emma dear." Uncle Sam said it so softly I doubted if Emma even heard him. She moved quickly around the kitchen where she started a fresh pot of coffee, sliced the gluten bread for toast and laid out the usual six strips of bacon.

"Uncle Sam's up," I said to Mama as she came down the backstairs and squeezed around me on my first step perch.

"Anyone with ears knows that Sam's up," Mama answered. "People as far as Mesquite can hear him yelling for Emma and his eye opener."

"What's an eye opener?" I asked, thinking how awful it must be to wake up with your eyes closed and have to swallow something to get them open.

Mama sighed. "It's that golden brown tonic in the glass next to the ice water." Then she added, "I'd just as soon you wouldn't say anything to your father about Sam's eye opener."

"I won't."

Then, defensively and with a burst of affection, Mama

32

added, "Sam's a gentleman. Notice how loud he yells for Emma . . . and then how politely he thanks her for coming in? Sam's all right. He never went to college like his brothers. Just stayed here with Mama and Papa and helped in the store. Julius drives a Cadillac and Ed drives a Chevrolet, but Sam never even learned how to drive a car. He's forty-five years old; he's got diabetes and has to watch his diet; he never goes anyplace exciting. . . . Well, not anyplace that *matters*. . . ." Mama skipped the details.

Every cab driver in Taro knew Sam's schedule. Every Sunday at two and every Wednesday evening at seven Sam took the interurban to Dallas. At one A.M., when the last interurban pulled into the Taro depot Sam was on it, but just barely. The driver usually went inside the coach and helped him off the train and into the cab. The drivers were gentle with him because, as Mama put it, Sam Levy was a gentleman. Even when he was unable to navigate he was cheerful and noncombative. The cab driver would always help him up the moonlit walk between the circles of flowers, lead him into his room, take the amount of the fare out of his wallet, then leave the front door locked and the key under the mat where he'd found it.

While Uncle Sam got dressed in the morning I'd watch Emma cook his breakfast. "Stay in here with Emma," she'd say to me. "It upsets Mistuh Sam if anyone hangs around before he's dressed and tested."

Whenever I asked Emma what she meant about Uncle Sam being tested she said, "Ask your mama." So I asked Mama and when I did she looked like she wished I hadn't.

"*Tested?*" Mama repeated. "I do wish Emma wouldn't—. Well, I've told you Uncle Sam has diabetes. That's why he has to eat gluten bread instead of Emma's good biscuits. Sam has to be careful not to take too much sugar. So he tests himself every morning and every night to see if he's OK."

"*How* does he test?" I persisted.

Mama looked uncomfortable. "Well, he has some litmus papers and some solutions and . . ." She suddenly changed the subject. "There's the mailman! Maybe he's got a letter from your father." She ran to the front door leaving me dangling in solutions and litmus papers.

The next morning I learned firsthand exactly how Uncle Sam tested himself. As soon as he had drunk his tonic and ice water he got out of bed and closed his bathroom door behind him. I was keyhole height and I peeked. The litmus paper was just colored paper, but I was totally unprepared for the solution part. It wasn't really a "solution" at all. It was —well, I was positive that neither Mama nor Emma knew for sure how Uncle Sam tested himself and I vowed that neither would ever learn from me!

At ten o'clock Uncle Sam pranced into the dining room and sat down at the head of the big oval table there. His round, full face was smooth and pink after his shave (and surely the tonic gave him a bit of color!), his orange hair was curly to the point of kinkiness even though he had plastered it down with bay rum. He wore a fresh shirt every morning and invariably a polka-dot bow tie. His silver belt buckle crowned the inflated bulge of his paunch like a stone in a platinum setting.

"Ready, I *say:* Ready, Emma!" he called. Then he pointed to a chair on his right and said amiably, "Sit down, Harry Lewis, and keep me company."

Emma brought in his gluten toast, three eggs sunny side up, and the six strips of crisp bacon. He made a bit to-do about putting saccharin in his coffee. "Can't eat sugar, boy. I *say:*

Can't eat sugar. Your Uncle Sam's got dia-bee-tees. Have to watch it like a hawk. Emma, bring this young man something to eat, and hurry up or I'll sic Ossie Honeycocker on you. I *say* . . ."

"I only have two hands, Mistuh Sam," Emma always muttered as she placed a sliced peach or a leftover biscuit with jam in front of me for my midmorning snack.

As he ate, Uncle Sam talked. He talked about the Levy store where he worked (but not too hard) every day, about Mama ("I *say:* Annie's got more than just visiting on her mind"), about his make-believe friend, Ossie Honeycocker, and about what a clannish family the Levys were. "Every one of 'em stayed right here on Levy Avenue and lived in style," he said. "Every one but Annie."

I learned from Uncle Sam that my grandfather helped build every church in Taro, that he acquired hundreds of acres of rich Texas black land with the profits from his general store, that he never charged his tenant farmers a penny more for their bacon or boots than he charged anyone else, that he cried the day he nailed up the entrance to his beloved opera house above his store, "I *say:* the Iroquois Theatre fire in Chicago scared him into it."

Uncle Sam had something nice to say about every member of the family, with the possible exception of Aunt Mamie, whom he never mentioned at all. Aunt Mamie hadn't spoken to Sam for five years, not since what Emma called "the terrible trouble." It seemed that Uncle Sam's name appeared on page one of the Monday Dallas *Morning News* in an account of a police raid on somebody's house where Uncle Sam happened to be at the time. Almost everybody forgave Sam and Uncle Julius fixed it up with the Dallas judge and kept it out of the Taro paper, but Aunt Mamie carried on about how Sam had disgraced the Levy name by being in "that vile place."

Uncle Sam took his time about eating, and I was glad.

"Ossie Honeycocker tells me that you are the smartest boy in the whole first-grade class at Sapulpa, Oklahoma. . . .

"Ossie Honeycocker can eat a whole goose at one sitting. I *say:* a *whole goose!* . . .

"Ossie Honeycocker is coming to Oklahoma one of these days to pay you a visit and I don't want your daddy walking Ossie's legs off on that crazy farm of his. . . ."

Ossie Honeycocker was the last word on everything. Uncle Sam would balance a bite of egg on a piece of gluten toast with one hand and shake the finger of his other hand at me. "I'll tell Ossie Honeycocker on you if you aren't good to your mama," he'd warn. "And Ossie Honeycocker will spank you—I *say:* he'll spank you right on your *ass!*" Then he'd pop the toast and egg into his mouth and chew violently while I got goose-pimply all over at the dirty word he'd used.

I never dared ask Uncle Sam whether Ossie Honeycocker was a man or a woman. I'm not sure he himself knew. He just loved the sound of those two words . . . Ossie Honeycocker . . . and I did, too.

Whenever I think of Uncle Sam I think of those late breakfasts and Ossie Honeycocker and the way he'd shout and giggle one minute and then be quiet and sort of sadlike the next. My little brother didn't interest him much and he seemed tongue-tied whenever my sisters spoke to him, but with me he never stopped. Most of what he said was nonsense, the kind of pure nonsense older people never speak to children any more. Where Uncle Julius and Aunt Mabel gave me dimes, Uncle Sam slipped me quarters, saying such things as, "Buy yourself some ice cream and buy some for

Ossie Honeycocker, too!" or "Go get yourself in trouble."
Once, Mama asked me what I was going to do with my
quarter and I told her Uncle Sam had suggested I "buy myself
a piece." She got very upset and said sternly, "Where's
Sam?" and went right to his room where she shut the door
behind her. She still looked mad when she came out. I had
to promise her I wouldn't mention "that word" to Papa when
we got home. I asked her what word and she said "piece."
"He meant *pie*, didn't he?" I asked her. "Why, of *course*,"
she said. I think she was relieved.

Mama went into action on the seventh day. After playing
hide-and-seek with Ed for a week the time had come for a
confrontation. Papa had called her the night before and
triggered her out of her Texas dreams and back to Oklahoma
reality.

"When in the hell are you coming home?"

"Is something wrong?" Mama asked.

"Nothing's *wrong*. I just can't find a dish or cup or glass
that isn't dirty."

Mama translated Papa perfectly. It was impossible for him
to say, "I miss you and the kids" because that was what he
really felt. He had to put her absence in terms of dirty dishes.
But she got the message.

I was sleepily conscious of Mama's stirrings around the
room at six in the morning. She dressed as carefully for her
interview as an actress dresses for a performance. She wore
her hair up high with her ears showing because that was the
way her brother liked her to wear it. Her dress was plain
(Ed hated anything showy) and she wore no jewelry except
her gold wedding band and her diamond earrings. For a
moment she wished her ears weren't pierced so she could

37

shed the earrings. Even a touch of affluence was a handicap when one went to Ed for money.

"Emma'll give you your breakfast," she whispered to me before she left. "As soon as Manny wakes up call your sisters at Aunt Josie's and tell them to come over and take care of him."

When Ed Levy stumbled into his kitchen for his morning coffee there was Annie, looking prettier than he remembered her. Aunt Nellie was sitting at the kitchen table drinking coffee while Mama was energetically moving around Nellie's kitchen sifting, pouring and stirring.

"Mornin', Ed," Mama said. "Even if you don't love me, I love you."

Ed grinned. He was one of the few men on earth who could still manage to look worried while he was grinning. "Now, Annie. You know I love you. I'm glad when you bring the kids to Taro for a visit. But there's one thing you've got to learn. The estate isn't made of money . . . even though Max Meyer thinks it is."

Mama didn't answer. Instead, she kept beating the pancake batter in the mixing bowl as though her life depended on it.

"What do you think you're doing?"

Mama put the bowl down and looked at her brother. Ed seemed older and tireder. The crow's feet around his eyes were furrowed deeper than ever. But his eyes were still bright and blue. Ed was the only Levy with blue eyes.

"Nellie asked me to come over and make some Oklahoma flapjacks for her and the boys and that's what I'm doing. Now if you want me to go, just say so."

Ed smiled. Annie had slipped in through the back door, caught him with his guard down and easily won round one.

"How much do you want this time?" he said, grinning worriedly.

This frontal counterattack surprised Mama so much she got flustered and spilled some of the batter on the floor. That gave Ed round two.

Aunt Nellie seemed to spring out of her chair. "I'll go wake up Alfred Ross and Philip Leon," she said quickly as she rushed out of the kitchen leaving brother and sister squared away for round three.

Mama had already been at Uncle Ed's for two hours when I watched Emma dash into Uncle Sam's room with his morning eye opener.

"Mistuh Sam's in a real good frame of mind this mornin'," Emma confided a few minutes later, as she turned the bacon strips and started the eggs.

"Is he happy because he tested good?" I asked.

"No-sir-ee," Emma said, giving a poke for each syllable to a new stick of wood in the firebox. "He's happy because it's Wednesday. Mistuh Sam always feels good on Wednesday, 'cause Wednesday night he goes to Dallas and then he *really* feels good."

I gave Uncle Sam a running start on his bacon and eggs before I opened the conversation. Then, digging into the half cantaloupe Emma had served me, I said, "Emma says you're going to Dallas tonight."

"Emma—I *say:* Emma talks too much."

"What do you do in Dallas, Uncle Sam?" I asked carefully.

He choked. His normally baby-pink morning face became a violent red. "Your mother's been over at Ed's a long time," he said. "Annie knows how to handle Ed. She's the smartest of us all. I *say:* Ed's always at the store by ten but his Chevy's still on the driveway. See it over there?"

"What do you do in Dallas?" I repeated.

"Damn it, I . . ." His hand was holding the handle of his coffee cup so tightly that he spilled a few drops on Emma's pristine tablecloth. "I visit friends."

"Do you see ole Ossie Honeycocker?"

"I do indeed," Uncle Sam said happily. "Ossie—I *say:* Ossie meets me at the interurban station every time I go to Dallas." He pointed at the window. "There goes Ed now. He's backing out of the drive."

I wasn't interested in Uncle Ed. I wanted to ask Uncle Sam a very important question but I couldn't get up the nerve.

"Wonder if Annie got all she wanted," he mused. "Hope so."

Impetuously I blurted out what was bothering me. "Will you take me with you, Uncle Sam? Please take me with you. I'll be a good boy."

Slowly, oh so slowly, Sam lowered his ready bite of egg on gluten toast and placed it back on his plate. He kept clasping and unclasping the handle of the cup. His hazel-green Levy eyes looked straight into mine.

"You want to go to Dallas with me?"

I said it as calmly as I could. "Yes."

"Tell me, Harry Lewis, what do you think Ossie and I do over there in Dallas?"

I remembered Papa's words by the Pullman car. "Screw around," I said. "Screw around and have fun."

His face was redder than I had ever seen it. He turned his eyes away from me and he began looking intently at the squares of rose and green and yellow reflected from the windowpanes onto the dining-room carpet. The colors seemed to hypnotize him. My innocence was so patent he couldn't get angry with me. But he was searching his mind for the one who (the son of a *bitch* who) had used that expression in front of a child. *Who?* Surely not Annie. Julius, maybe. Or Emma. Or Varney. Or Mabel, even.

"Please, Uncle Sam. Will you . . . *please?*"

"Will he what?" Mama asked, walking into the dining room. She could see that Uncle Sam was flabbergasted about something, so she said to me, "Better go upstairs and tell your sisters I'm back. Let your Uncle Sam finish his breakfast in peace."

"I just asked if I could—"

"He wants to go to Dallas," Sam said hastily, before I could use my borrowed phrase again. "He wants to ride the interurban."

"We're going to Dallas, all right, but not on the interurban. Julius is going to drive us. We're catching the sleeper for home tonight."

"So soon?" Sam asked.

"Max needs me. You won't forget to put out the suits you promised for the Salvation Army?"

"I won't forget. The war—I *say:* the war must be over. Who won . . . Ed?"

Mama shook her head.

"Did *you* win, Annie? Good!" He repeated it. "Good!" He spoke slowly. "You deserve more than any of us, Annie, and I'll tell you *why.* You had the guts—I *say: guts* to break away. You were the only Levy who had the guts to—" His voice broke and he turned to humor for his recovery. "You're also more deserving because you have to live with Max. Anyway, I'm glad you won."

Mama laughed. Impulsively, she walked over to where

Uncle Sam was sitting at the table and she stood real close to him and gave him a long hug. Then she bent over and kissed him on the forehead.

"I love you, Sam," she said. "You don't demand anything from anybody. Maybe you're weak, but I love you most of all."

Uncle Sam, for once, had nothing to say. He took out his fresh handkerchief and blew his nose.

Mama straightened up. "Ed didn't win. I didn't win, either. Max won."

In a way, so had I. Uncle Sam gave me a five-dollar bill when I kissed him good-bye. He said that Ossie—I *say:* Ossie Honeycocker wanted me to have it.

2. Tight Shoe Night

We spotted Papa long before the train had stopped. As soon as the porter had taken off the luggage and placed it in a neat row on the red brick apron alongside the track we jumped, one by one, into Papa's arms and he squeezed us hard before he put us down. Mama, holding Manny, was the last one off. Papa took Manny from her, placed him on the ground by the rest of us, then lifted Mama two feet in the air in a typical Papa hug. He kissed her on the mouth a couple of times. (Mama and Papa always kissed their children and each other on the mouth. A cheek kiss meant they were mad about something.)

Ernie Cooper, Papa's stonemason, driver, yardman, bodyguard and confidant, was putting the suitcases into our car. Papa had a thing about cars. They didn't have to be new and they didn't have to function perfectly but they had to be big. This one was a 1918 Packard of frayed gentility whose long, crimped hood and radiator front gave it "the Rolls Royce look."

Mama smiled at Ernie, then whispered to Papa, "He's sober. How did you manage that?"

"He says he's not going to get drunk until the drouth ends," Papa whispered back.

"Now I've heard everything."

The girls sat up front with Ernie, and Papa sat in the back seat with Mama, Manny and me. He kept chattering about one thing after another: Oil people were nosing around the ranch for possible drilling sites, his Super Gigantic Money Raising Sale at the store was going strong, Sapulpa was getting a new glass factory . . . but he didn't fool Mama.

Mama laughed. "Stop being nervous," she said. "I got your money."

Papa stopped talking long enough for me to hear what Ernie was telling my sisters about the Indians having a special pow-wow last night where they danced their Rain Dance and prayed for rain. Then, slowly, incredulously, Papa inquired, "*All* of it? Did he give you . . . *five?*"

"You don't know Ed," Mama said matter-of-factly. "I asked for ten. He swore that eight would ruin him. So I did him a favor and took six."

Papa was stunned. "*Six?*"

"And don't go thinking of more land to buy with the other thousand," Mama said, reading his mind. "I earned it and I get to spend it." She changed the subject. "About those dirty dishes. Where was Beulah?"

"Beulah sent word she's sick. She's not sick, Annie. She's mad. You'll have to get her back."

"Mad?"

Papa looked sheepish. "I had a little—*don't fly off the handle, Annie darlin'!*—party. Just Judge Wright and Fred Patrick and Vance Likely and some of the boys for poker. It kinda got out of hand. Beulah came to work the next morning, took one look and left. That wasn't right, was it?"

Mama, who relied on Beulah and respected her judgment, asked cautiously, "What did she see when she took one look? Was somebody dead?"

Papa spat. He never liked to hear talk of dying, even in jest, so he canceled the evil implications with good saliva. "That's no way to talk, Annie. You know how Fred drinks whiskey—a whole glassful at a time without stopping. Well, he ate too much corned beef and couldn't make it to the bathroom and . . . got . . . sick . . . on the hall rug."

"Look out the window and wave at people," Mama said to me severely. She spoke to Papa in a businesslike way. "What did they break? I know they broke *something*. What did they break?"

"Now, Annie, I'm tellin' you the truth. Don't you appreciate the truth? It wasn't a wild party. I don't smoke and I don't drink and I don't run around with—uh—*you* know. And I *am* telling you the honest truth. I just asked some of the boys over and—"

"What did they break?"

"Your cut-glass lamp."

"No." She said the word softly, which meant it hurt. The lamp was her favorite possession.

"Vance doesn't know how he did it. He musta got caught in the cord somehow. He wants to buy you another one but I won't let him do it. Besides, you've got that extra thousand dollars. You can use it to buy a cut-glass lamp and another set of dishes and . . ." Papa said the next words so fast they were barely intelligible. "A new livingroomrug."

Mama started to cry. It wasn't just the mess she was approaching, nor what she would have to spend, nor even

45

Papa's bullheadedness. It was Ed's silly preoccupation with money, and poor Sam's wasted life, and Julius having to be without Miss Alice, and Mabel's useless cedar chests and now this.

"Two fifteen South Oak!" Ernie Cooper called out as he turned the cumbersome car into the driveway. The house looked fine from the outside but when she imagined what it looked like inside Mama started to weep louder. Ernie was putting the luggage on the front porch (Papa was itching to ask what Mama had in all those boxes but he didn't dare), my sisters were hugging Junior, our hound dog, and I had raced halfway down the block to say hello to my friend Billy Longmire. Ernie Cooper was holding Manny and the front-door key. Papa was standing by the car with the door open waiting for Mama to step out, but she just pushed deeper into the back seat and cried a while.

And then the front door opened and Beulah in her white starched apron was on the front porch with a grin for Mama and a glare for Papa. She shooed my sisters into the house, took Manny in her arms, and walked briskly to the car. "You can come on in now, Miz Meyer. The worst is over."

I never understood why Mama was always running off to the ranch with Papa at the oddest times. When Papa would come back from market in New York or Chicago he'd hardly get our presents unpacked before he'd say, "Come with me to the farm, Annie. Let's see what's goin' on out there." The funny thing was that Mama, who wasn't one bit interested in farming, always went.

Sure enough, Mama had no sooner put her purse on the dresser and placed a runner over the big burned hole in the front-room rug than Papa said, "Annie, I've got to drive

46

Ernie back to the farm. Want to come with me? I've got something I want to show you." His voice sounded over-casual, distant, as though his mind was someplace else.

Mama was still in her best silk dress and she hadn't begun to unpack our clothes and if you asked me she didn't want to drive the five miles to the ranch right then in the middle of the morning, but she looked at Papa like she felt sorry for him and said, "Beulah'll look after the kids. A little fresh air will do us both good."

Ernie drove and Papa sat in the back seat with Mama, holding her hand. The car windows were cranked down as far as they would go and while there was a good breeze it was stinging hot. Mama looked sadly at the parched land, brown and crusty with only an occasional patch of faded green.

"It's a real drouth," Papa said. "The ponds are drying up. One hundred and five degrees yesterday. Just as hot today."

"Don't worry," Ernie yelled optimistically from the front seat. "The Indians danced real good last night. It'll rain for sure." He pointed to the west. "Cloud over there. *Could be.* That Rain Dance never misses." His eyes misted as his imagination led the cloud to rain and the rain to whiskey.

POW!

The car veered off to one side and Ernie wrestled with the steering wheel to keep it on the road. "Blowout!" he announced as the Packard careened for a few yards, then skidded to a stop on the narrow shoulder between the road and the ditch. "Right front tire!"

It was an old story to Mama who glared at Papa and asked crossly, "Why don't you buy a decent set of tires?"

Papa tried to soothe her. "Ernie'll change the flat. Won't

47

take ten minutes. Sun's gone behind a cloud. Won't be as hot."

But hot it was. Hot and increasingly humid as it appeared that the prayers for rain were going to be answered. Mama's silk dress was sticking to her and her sewed-in shields were beginning to reach the saturation point.

Ernie Cooper called Papa out of the car and said to him in a low and troubled voice, "Max, the spare's in your garage on Oak Street. Forgot to put it back in the car last time I fixed it." And then, apropos of nothing at all, he added, "I could sure as hell use a snort."

"Can we run on the rim the rest of the way?" Papa asked.

"It'll ruin the wheel. Two miles to town. I'll walk."

Papa knew too well Ernie's danger signals. If Ernie left for town now he'd not see him again until he bailed him out of jail three days and a hundred snorts later. "We'll stay right here, Ernie. Someone's bound to stop and give us a lift to town."

"Annie, dear—" Papa began.

"Shut up," Mama snapped. "I heard you. The flat's here, the tire's at home, and you're *happy*."

It wasn't the first time Mama had accused Papa of purposely buying rotten tires or forgetting spares. She was convinced that he enjoyed breaking down on the road so he could have the fun of being rescued. He was constantly bringing strangers into the house in town or the farmhouse and entertaining them with food and drink because they had stopped to help him. Face it: It was one way of meeting people.

"What are you doing?" Papa gasped.

"I'm taking off this dress before it's ruined," Mama answered. "Tell Ernie to stand behind the car. Don't just stare at me!

48

Help me pull it over my head . . . and don't you dare tear it!"

Any sort of public disrobing bothered Papa, and Mama's removing her dress in broad daylight put him in a state of mild shock.

"Don't look so disgraced, Max. My princess slip covers me as much as a dress." She would have liked to hang the damp dress outside in the wind but she thought better of that and folded it neatly over the back of the front seat.

Two or three cars passed them but despite Papa's and Ernie's gesticulations they refused to stop.

"It's not nearly as hot as it was when we left," Papa said cheerfully.

"I smell rain," Ernie said. He smelled more than rain.

"Let it rain," Mama said, removing her shoes and rolling her wet stockings off. "I'm almost comfortable."

Papa was more upset at Mama's sudden good-naturedness than he'd been when she was chewing nails. When she invited him to join her and remove his shirt, shoes and socks he acted pained and stuffy.

The first raindrops had just begun to plaster the dust on the road into dark wet splotches when Papa spotted the approaching Winton, which he immediately recognized as belonging to Melvin Smith, the county judge.

"Quick, Annie! Put on your dress!" Papa commanded. "It's Judge Smith and his wife."

"Do I look like Houdini?" Mama said irritably. "I couldn't wriggle inside that sticky dress in an hour, much less a half minute. Relax. Judge Smith sees Emily in her slip every day of the week."

The rain was increasing. It was becoming a thick, jungle-like downpour, so hot and acrid that wisps of steam began to form in some of the low places in the fields.

"Maybe he won't see us," Papa said hopefully. "Maybe he'll just drive on by."

"Drive on *by?*" Mama was shocked now. "Max Meyer: If you don't get out there and wave the Smiths down, I'll do it myself!"

Papa knew she would, so he stuck his head out into the hot, peppery rain and waved. Judge Smith had been barely inching along and when he saw who was waving at him he managed to stop just a few yards down the highway. He backed up, rolled his window down and yelled, "Hello, Max!"

Papa ran across the road and ducked into the Smith car to fill them in. Meanwhile, Mama had put her hand on her pretty dress with an idea of putting it on, but when she considered the gymnastics involved, plus the fact it surely would be ruined if she got out in the rain with it on, she replaced it on the seat, settled back and appeased her frustrations by wiggling her toes.

Papa was drenched by the time he got back into the Packard. "The Smiths are going to drive you and Ernie back to the house," he panted. "Ernie will get the tire and the Judge will drive him back here."

"Can't Ernie stay?" Mama whispered, pointing at Ernie in the front seat, lost in boozy dreaming. She tried to sound cooperative because she felt sorry for Max with his hair wetted down flat and his face dripping water as if he were taking a shower bath.

"If I leave Ernie here," Papa whispered back so Ernie couldn't hear him, "he'll never stay and he's gotta fix that tire. The Judge is going to leave Mrs. Smith at our house and sit right on top of Ernie until he does what he's supposed to do."

Mama saw how hard Papa was trying. "Anything you say, dear," she said encouragingly.

We were in front of our house in just a few minutes. While Beulah went for the umbrella she found my bathing suit and told me to get into it. I got to run out in the rainstorm and take the umbrella to Mama and Mrs. Smith who were in the garage now with the Judge and Ernie. Mama made Mrs. Smith use the umbrella while Mama ran right out into the rain and down the driveway.

After the ladies were in the house drinking lemonade and the Judge's car had gone to rescue Papa, Mama laughed as she replayed for us her barefoot dash through the downpour in her princess slip. "It all seems silly now," she said. "The rain's beginning to let up. See, Emily," Mama said to Mrs. Smith who was a fellow member of the Sapulpa Shakespeare Club, "It's turning into Portia's 'gentle rain from heaven.'"

Mrs. Smith nodded. Club members were encouraged to quote Shakespeare whenever possible and she followed Mama's lead. "Out there on the highway it looked like 'the rain that raineth every day.' It was *awful*."

It wasn't fifteen minutes before Judge Smith had returned and was honking for his wife to come out to their car. The rain had almost stopped. Mama tried to get the Judge to come in for some refreshments but he said he couldn't because he was late for Court.

It was almost noontime before Papa appeared.

"I had to take Ernie to the ranch and turn him over to his missus," Papa said. "Kate's the only one who can hold him down when he gets the hankerin'."

We children had already eaten, but because we'd been away for a week Mama let all of us sit around the dining-room table while Papa ate his dinner. "I'm really not very hungry," he said as Beulah brought in a generous encore of boiled brisket, a second refill of new potatoes and garden peas, and a third plate of steaming, crispy corn bread.

When dinner was over and Mama had sent all of us to the sleeping porch for a nap I heard Papa say in that same faraway voice he had used earlier, "Annie, I still want to show you that . . . uh . . . project out at the ranch. Feel like tryin' a second time? The road's cool now from the rain, so the tires won't blow. Car's in the garage, ready. Uh . . . ?"

I'm darned if Mama wasn't foolish enough to say the same thing she said the first time. "A little fresh air will do us both good."

Whenever Mama went to the Salvation Army headquarters she took me with her. Our visits there were private trans-actions between Mama and me. Papa knew vaguely that Mama took things to the Salvation Army but he had no idea how involved she really was in the lives of Major and Mrs. Miller and their wards. Mama preferred it this way be-cause she knew how Papa was built.

"Your father's generous to a fault," Mama said to me.

"Does that mean he's too generous?"

"You can't be too generous," Mama said emphatically. "But generosity, like everything else, can be abused. Sometimes people ask for help who don't need or deserve it."

"It's not the fool who asks . . ." I suggested.

"Right!" Mama said, pleased that I had remembered one of her pet expressions. "It's the fool who gives. And sometimes we give to the wrong people and the wrong causes. Your father can't resist a hard-luck story, even when it's invented. That's foolish generosity."

"Then why don't we talk about the Salvation Army in front of Papa? The Army isn't foolish, is it?"

"Good heavens, no!" Mama said. "I'll try to explain it to you in a way you'll understand. Y'see, your father is very religious even if he doesn't know a whole lot about religion. He designed and built the Jewish temple in Sapulpa and made it easy for anybody who wanted to worship there to come and do so without worrying about cost. You know how he puts it: no dues, no fees. He says his Old Testament prayers and he believes God is the one and only Supreme Being."

"Isn't he?" I asked.

Mama hesitated. "If your father says so, I guess He is." She proceeded slowly. "But a great many people, including Major and Mrs. Miller and all the Salvation Army corps, believe that there is another Supreme Being named Jesus Christ and they pray to Him, too. They follow the Old Testament just as your father does, but they follow the New Testament, too, and your father doesn't do that."

"Who's right?" I asked.

"Don't tell Papa I said this," Mama confided, "but they *both* are. I can't see where it matters so much if someone doesn't believe the way you do. What matters is the way that person lives. Is he good? Is he honest? Is he kind? There are lots of teachings in that New Testament which your father practices even if he doesn't think he believes in them: Love thy neighbor as thyself, blessed are the merciful, suffer little children to come unto me, things like that."

Mama didn't usually talk about religion, but now that I had asked her she was telling me her concept of the way it was. It was the only time in my whole life that she spoke so fully on the subject.

"Papa is a Jew," she said. "So am I. So are you. We were born of Jewish parents. We are Jews by birth as well as Jews by religion. The Old Testament is the Jewish Bible. Jews pray only to God. Some Jews think they are better than other people because they are Jewish. They think the Jews are right and everybody else is wrong.

"But the Millers and your teachers and most of our neighbors and friends are Christians. They love the New Testament as we do the Old. They pray to God but they also pray to Jesus. Some of them, too, think that they are the only ones who are right and everybody else is wrong.

"I say that the Jews aren't better than the Christians and the Christians aren't better than the Jews. I think that if people just do the best they can all the time and help the poor in purse and the poor in spirit they'll go to heaven, whether they're Jews or Christians or . . . nothing at all."

"Then, Mama . . ." My voice was low and full of embarrassment. "When Major Miller or one of the corps prays 'in Jesus's name' . . . is it all right if I say Amen?"

I didn't understand why Mama felt impelled to give me a quick hug at that particular moment but she did. "Honey, you can say Amen whenever you feel like it."

"And when the others sing the song, 'Jesus will help us to conquer the foe' . . . can I sing it, too?"

"Absolutely," Mama affirmed to my great relief. "It doesn't matter if the song is "Onward, Christian Soldiers" or "Onward, Jewish Soldiers," it's the *spirit* that counts. And if your father insists on spitting every time he hears the words Jesus Christ —well, he's mixing his religion with superstition and people who do that are just . . . just plain damned fools."

Mama believed in the Salvation Army because she saw with her own eyes the good they did. They opened their doors to the hungry, the sick, the down-and-out. They didn't expect miracles but they often performed them.

I learned early that not everyone respected the Army as much as Mama did. Many people were condescending to the organization and some were openly critical. They parodied the Army's songs and prayers with:

> Hallelujah, I'm a bum;
> Hallelujah, bum again.
> Hallelujah, give us a handout
> To revive us again.

Through my many visits with Mama to the squat, red brick Salvation Army Hut I had learned that there was more than a "handout" there. Many who came just to get a free meal or a bed for the night found something they hadn't bargained for; they found the kind of generosity Mama respected and they responded to it in kind. I was too young to understand why and how the Salvation Army changed people for the better but I knew they did.

It troubled me when some of my classmates would tease the Army children. Billy Bledsoe's father blew the trumpet in the corps and I knew Billy from our visits to the Hut. Billy was older than I was, a fourth grader. When the Washington School children ganged up on him at recess and yelled, "Put a penny on the drum!" he didn't yell back because Captain Bledsoe had told him not to. But I did. When a sixth grader shouted, "Salvation Army, save my soul, I'm gonna go to heaven on a telephone pole!" I took my life in my hands and ran right up to him and stood under his chin with my fists clenched shouting, "The Salvation Army's got the right to beat the drum . . . Join the Army, Brother, and see the devil run!" I am convinced that the only reason he didn't push my face in was his complete bewilderment at seeing a Jewish boy (who had his own troubles with the bullies) battling for the wrong army.

Major Miller himself came for the boxes Mama had brought from Texas, and drove Mama and me to the Salvation Army Hut in his truck. Mrs. Major Miller met us outside and helped carry the things into the office. Mama was especially fond of Mrs. Miller and they were on a first-name basis, Marian and Annie, when they were alone. Marian's husband was always Major Miller to Mama. Surely she knew his given name but she didn't use it.

Mama admired Major Miller for many reasons but she talked most about his attitude toward women. At a time when women were excluded from many professions and reminded that their "place was in the home," Major Miller regarded women as the equal of men in all except physical force. At least once a day he repeated the words of William Booth, founder of the Army: "My best men are women." Mama never failed to read aloud to me the placard on Major Miller's office wall that said, "Woman is the equal to man in the value of her gifts . . . and if she is given a fair chance she will prove it to be so."

It hadn't occurred to Mama that Major Miller would turn down Uncle Sam's gray, herringbone suit. At Mama's insistence he did try it on and it fit surprisingly well, but as the Major himself put it, "I feel like a banker when I'm dressed like this, and I'm not too crazy about bankers." When he got back into his dark blue coat with the gold buttons down the front and the Army cap with its shiny visor and red ribbon even Mama had to admit he looked more like the Major Miller she knew.

She did persuade Marian Miller to accept one or two of Aunt Mabel's undergarments, but everything else Mama brought from Taro was either sold or given away: terms that are interchangeable when the seller/giver is the Salvation Army.

"It's time for choir practice," Major Miller said to Mama. "Stay a while . . . please."

He knew Mama would stay. She always did. I suspected that she timed our visits to coincide with what Major Miller called "choir practice." She loved the songs they sang but she loved even more the way they sang them. To Mama, the Salvation Army sang with real love and dedication. Night after night they paraded up Dewey Avenue to where it intersected Main Street. There, in front of the City Drug Store, they held their prayer meetings. Cars honked their horns (some on purpose), people walked in front of them, smart alecks shouted at them or even pushed them, but if the marchers were aware of these disturbances they did not show it. "Onward, Christian soldiers" they sang as Major Miller led the way, his head high, his baritone voice on pitch . . . "Marching as to war . . . With the cross of Jesus . . . Going on before!"

Directly behind Major Miller in the procession was Old Fats. Nobody ever called him anything except Fats or Old Fats. Old Fats was the perennial Salvation Army Christmas Santa Claus. The local group's motheaten red-velvet costume fit him without a smidgin of stuffing. The only make-up he needed was whiskers. Fats must have eaten prodigious quantities of food because his stomach was enormous, but he was one of those fat men who handle themselves deftly.

His shirt collar was always white and starched, his uniform pressed, his shoes shined. Even as he marched in the parade pounding the worn, black heart of the taut drumskin with his uncompromising beat he looked clean and neat, almost dandified.

Behind Fats and his drum were four of the corps in a row: an emaciated man named Steve who was as skinny as the tubes of his trombone, Teresa, a black-haired, olive-skinned part-Indian girl who rhythmically clapped a thick tambourine, Captain Bledsoe who tried (and sometimes failed) to make the notes come out in the right order from his spittle-clogged cornet, and white-haired Corporal Mary Wade, a motherly soul who mated a pair of brass cymbals so respectfully they clanged but did not clash. Mrs. Major Miller, clutching copies of the Salvation Army magazine, *War Cry*, sang and marched on the last row, her eyes straight ahead.

The rehearsal known as choir practice took place in a small room between the office and the men's dormitory. Here new songs were learned and old ones sung for sheer joy. I remember one that went

> Come, join our Army, to battle we go;
> Jesus will help us to conquer the foe;
> Fighting for right and opposing the wrong;
> The Salvation Army is marching along.

Another one of our favorites was called "Somebody's Girl." Everybody including the audience would join in on the chorus with the words, "Throw out the life line."

Mama's favorite was called "O Boundless Salvation." She always looked at me and smiled when they began to sing it because she knew I would join in. How I loved that song!

O boundless salvation! Deep ocean of love,
O fulness of mercy, Christ brought from above,
The whole world redeeming, so rich and so free,
Now flowing for all men, come roll over me!

Every time we sang that song I took it literally and saw myself standing waist-deep in the ocean, with the waves rolling over me (but not knocking me down).

The Millers walked us to the door, and Mama dropped a few steps behind me while she spoke in a lowered voice to Marian Miller. Mama was concerned about Teresa.

"She's so beautiful. She has the look of a . . . an angel!"

"Too beautiful," Marian Miller said sadly. "She'd be a lot better off if she'd been born ugly. Men ruined her. She was more dead than alive when we found her. And the baby—" She didn't finish. Mama must have known the story because she nodded.

"And Steve—?" Mama asked.

Steve, the trombone player, was the puzzlement of Mama and the Millers. He blew his horn, prayed and sang regularly, and never caused a disturbance at the Hut. But Steve had the disconcerting habit of pocketing twenty cents from the collection plate every Saturday night. No more, no less— and only on Saturdays.

"He's such a *steady* man," Mama said. "I don't see how he can do it. Don't you ever confront him?"

"Occasionally," Marian Miller sighed. "And when we do he always admits his guilt and gives the money back. But I live for the day when he will bring it to us of his own volition—or better yet, conquer the sinful impulse to take what isn't his. Until then, we'll wait it out."

When Major Miller offered to drive us home in the Army

truck Mama thanked him but insisted on our walking. "We're going to the store," she said. "It's just a few blocks." And then, as she shook his hand, she managed to leave some folded bills in it.

"You shouldn't, Sister Annie," the Major said quietly. "You do so much for us."

Mama blushed and fumbled for words whenever Major Miller called her Sister Annie. "Texas money," she said, half apologetically. "You might say I found it."

She grabbed my hand and started for the sidewalk. Steve was standing on the curb. Mama smiled pleasantly and I waved good-bye to him. "Don't take any wooden nickels," he called affably. Mama's smile congealed into a simper. She and I were thinking the same thing: Would Steve take four wooden nickels to make his weekly twenty cents?

About a half block from the Hut Mama said, "It embarrasses me when a fine man like Major Miller has to thank people for helping others." We walked up Dewey without speaking to each other and then Mama said, "I hope Max doesn't ask where we've been." As we turned the corner by the City Drug and headed toward Papa's store she added, "What your father doesn't know won't hurt him."

Mama was never as impressed with Papa's store as he wanted her to be. She encouraged him in his merchandising endeavors and she often helped out but her heart wasn't in it. Papa blamed her indifference on the fact that her own father had had a much larger store with more employees and more business. Mama insisted that a peripatetic husband and four active children were a full-time job. Perhaps the real reason was that Mama feared if she showed more than a passing interest in the store Papa would delegate to her the running of it while he spent all of his time elsewhere. "As it is," she said, "he's always someplace else. He's buying cattle or looking at more land or making an oil and gas lease or eating bananas at the Farmer's Exchange." She knew that the only way she could cope with him was to maintain a mobility of her own. Cleverly, she refused to be tied down.

Papa liked the merchant role but he was too restless to live up to his own merchant image. He couldn't stand the inactivity of waiting for customers. He would start tearing out cabinets or moving dress racks or rearranging the shoe department to use up his nervous energy. He ripped up all the flooring and had a new hardwood floor installed. He tore out the whole back wall of the building and put in plate glass for "the daylight look." He moved merchandise from the main floor to the bargain basement until the clerks were dizzy. With Papa around there had to be movement.

At the extreme rear of the store Papa built an open cashier's cage and office on a kind of platform island. It resembled a gun emplacement. One had to climb a half-dozen steps to reach it but once there one could survey everything that was going on on the main floor. "Excellent security against shoplifters," Papa said.

Since the money was in this elevated pillbox, Papa then had to construct a network of lines and pulleys upon which wire baskets were transported from the various departmental stations below to the lofty office where change was made and purchases sacked. Gravity took the baskets back to their starting points.

Mama thought the office on stilts was silly and she did everything in her power to make it ineffectual. She pointed out that one might spot a shoplifter, all right, but by the time one ran down the steps and ran to the front of the store to apprehend the thief, he'd be gone. As for the baskets, Mama said, "You have to work harder to get the change than you did to make the sale." She was constantly creating false alarms. She would haul sacks of groceries or empty boxes in the baskets. Once she pullied a brick to the cashier. Another time she hid behind an open umbrella and sent a message in the basket which read: SEND DOWN ALL THE CASH OR I'LL SHOOT TO KILL. The cashier, Mrs. Sparks, almost fainted.

But if Mama disliked the trolley system of cashiering she dearly loved Papa's vast premium department. Premiums were rewards for purchases and customers saved their sales tickets until they had enough to choose the premium they wanted. While there were candlesticks, bookends, picnic baskets, cameras, Thermos jugs, toys, dolls and dozens of other premium choices, Mama leaned toward pitcher-and-tumbler sets. The local glass factory specialized in these sets and Papa bought them for premiums by the gross. It might stretch the imagination to call these sets "hand painted" (as Papa did) but they were lavishly decorated. Both pitcher and tumbler were enormous and were (in Papa's own words) "pure glass."

Mama played Lady Bountiful with these sets. She loved picking up a cardboard box containing a pitcher and eight glasses and giving it to someone she liked. "So nice for lemonade," she'd say, refusing the bundle of accumulated sales tickets. "Use them for something else."

Papa, who thought nothing of buying a white-faced calf for $150 and selling it for $15, went berserk when Mama gave away one of his premium glass sets. He'd swell up like a balloon, dash down the steps to the bargain basement and swear a lot as he paced the floor. He probably beat his breast, too.

Papa prided himself on his "organization." By organization he meant that he had the pleasure of starting everything and his staff had the job of carrying it through to completion. He would travel to St. Louis, Chicago or New York and make carload purchases—usually of items that were on their way out of fashion or already outmoded. Just when men were insisting on collar-attached shirts, he bought six thousand collarless ones at thirty-five cents each and twelve thousand collars to go with them at two cents each. The shirts were all the same pongeelike material—*and all the same color,* a muddy yellow some people call "puce." The collars, unfortunately, didn't match the shirts. They were green, purple and cream colored—but as Papa philosophized, "You can't have everything." The wholesaler who was stuck with them assured Papa that the shirts would "wear like iron" and on that point he was correct. Twenty years later people were still using those shirts as diapers, dust cloths, bandannas, or sashes . . . but you could never mistake that puce color. It stood for a Max Meyer "buy"—and it wore like iron.

Another "buy" was a shipment of one thousand knee-length ladies' fur-trimmed coats after hemlines had dropped almost to the ankle. Papa found out it was harder to sell a short coat when styles were long than a long coat when styles were short, but somehow he managed to sell them all. Men's belted-back suits (when plain backs were "in"), men's wide-brimmed hats (when narrow brims prevailed), women's long-waisted dresses (when short-waists were in vogue) . . . these were typical of Papa's creative carload buying.

To sell his buys he covered the show windows with

lurid signs proclaiming PRICES CUT TO THE BONE or WARE-
HOUSE PURCHASE SALE or 10¢ ON-THE-DOLLAR VALUES. He hired
itinerant sales promoters who dreamed up enticing circu-
lars, which were left at every front door in the county. His
staff of salespeople were experts at swimming against the current and selling people what they didn't know they wanted.

Papa would stir up all that excitement, get the thrill of
handing presents to the first fifty customers, give his staff
a rousing pep talk, then spend the rest of the day at the
ranch where Ernie Cooper was building tourist cottages
out of what Papa called "natural stone." He'd return at the
end of the day just in time to check up, lock the front
door and go home.

"I wish you liked the store better," he'd say wistfully to
Mama. "You're a better salesman than I am!" This was a
superb compliment because Papa knew how to get customers
so confused they'd buy anything.

Mama could sell, all right. She used a lot of psychology.
She'd act as if she didn't care a bit whether or not she
made the sale. Papa called her approach the don't-give-
a-damn system—but it worked. Customers actually bought
just to spite her. But Mama did give a damn. If she found
she wasn't succeeding in her original approach she'd throw
psychology out the window and start price cutting.

CUSTOMER: How much for that child's coat?
MAMA: $12.98.
CUSTOMER: Not today.
MAMA: How about $10?
CUSTOMER: We'll be back later.
MAMA: $8?
CUSTOMER: But—

MAMA: $7?
CUSTOMER: You make it hard to say no.
MAMA: $6.50? That's half price.
CUSTOMER: Oh—wrap it up.

Mama didn't always show a profit but she sure as hell moved merchandise.

When Papa got wind of Mama's desperation sales tactics he exploded. "What's the good of an organization? Why have a store when you give things away?" Sometimes he would throw a regular tantrum and break one of the display premium pitchers (invariably one that was already cracked). He'd take the stairs to the basement two at a time and scream a lot down there until he felt better.

Why did Mama behave in the store as she did? Spite, perhaps, spite for Papa's leaving everything to his caged organization while he ran free outside. Or perhaps she figured that Papa would stick closer to his business if he knew Mama was marking down the markup in his absence. She noticed, too, that when she pulled her price-cutting shenanigans Papa wasn't nearly so insistent about her spending more time in the store.

If one may use the luxury of hindsight, Mama's motives were clear as crystal. Customer baiting was a game with her because she possessed the ability to see beyond the sale, beyond the "organization," beyond Papa's darned-fool baskets, his premiums and his carload buys. She refused to take these things seriously because she somehow knew that the store would never be their sole means of livelihood. The first oil wells were already coming in and she was sure there would be many more. There would be money enough without having to beg a customer to buy a coat for $12.98. And besides . . . couldn't Max see? If worst came to worst (it couldn't happen—but if it *did*), if instead of oil wells they got dry holes, if nobody wanted Papa's bargains . . . why, they could always go back to Taro. It would hurt her pride and Max wouldn't like it, but it was a good feeling, knowing that her family would always have plenty to eat. Uncle Sam had said it. Mama was the smartest of them all.

Saturday night was "tight shoe night." It was also dress-up night, spend-money night, get-drunk night. It was the crescendo and climax, the time most of these people on the crowded streets had waited for all week long. Stores were open until nine o'clock and from sundown on you couldn't find a parking space on or near the T formed at the top by Main Street and vertically by Dewey Avenue. Vacant lots seven and eight blocks from town were packed with trucks and pickups and model Ts and beat-up Chevys and fifth-hand Dodges. And even farther away from the main drag were wagons whose teams were tethered near hay and water and whose beds would be crowded with sleeping youngsters when families headed back to the farms after the stores were closed. First, though, the parents and children —wedged tightly against each other for protection from jostlers —walked past the lighted store windows, dreamed ownership dreams, and stuffed themselves with popcorn, all-day suckers, ice cream cones and licorice sticks.

Saturday night was dust. It settled on the straw-and-ribbon brims of women's hats, it matted hair, lodged in children's ears and clung to dogs who couldn't shake it off. Sudden gusts of hot wind caused the dust to swirl in eddies down the sidewalk and kept merchants busy sweeping the entrances and front interiors of their stores.

Saturday night was noise. Horns honked interminably as drivers crept along Dewey or Main looking for nonexistent parking spaces. Double parkers jammed traffic despite noisy protests against them. Millions of buzzing insects slapped and swarmed around the signs and street lamps. Phonograph records blared from Harmony Music and the Oklahoma Supply. Pipeline workers and cowboys, encouraged by the beers under their belts, shouted obscenities at each other. There was every conceivable kind of argument, and each of them was loud: between husbands and wives, between farmhands and whores, between tanked-up men primed for brawls, between kids who just wanted to holler at each other because it was Saturday night.

This night was different from all other nights in an Oklahoma town. Sunday's sun would shine on fresh collars and scrubbed necks, on bowed heads and pure thoughts . . . but Saturday night belonged, at least in part, to the devil. Men and boys said aloud the dirty things they only thought about the rest of the week and women's bodies parted company with their minds. Taverns and bars had the sweet stink of hair tonic, cheap perfume, sweat, cigarette smoke, tobacco juice (both in and out of cuspidors), beer, burps and belches.

Since Oklahoma was still morally bound by old Indian Territory rules, hard liquor was illegal. The beer was 3.2 and harmless enough, but somebody always knew somebody else who knew somebody else with a pint of corn whiskey from Pushmataha County. On Saturday night you swallowed anything you could lay your hands on to make you feel good, even homemade wine that was still green. It didn't matter a lot what you drank because you always got sick and threw up before the night was over.

There were certain zones that "nice people" avoided—like Earl's Domino and Beer Joint and the Red Man Bar. And there were subtly special spots that looked all right but weren't really: the street alongside the Empress Theatre, and the side entrance to the St. James Hotel and the dimly lit hallways where flyspecked signs said ROOMS but did not hint at what went on in those rooms at the top of the steep, dark flights of stairs. Children thought nothing of walking in front of these places any day of the week, but on Saturday night they instinctively took the other side of the street.

Over the whole downtown area on these hot, dusty, noisy summer Saturday nights was a kind of chemical aura that could neither be seen nor touched but which intensely affected many of the grownups. If a passerby on a crowded Saturday night happened to glance down the dark alley behind Orrick's Furniture Store he might see two writhing figures, one of them pinned by consent to the building wall. Nor was it advisable to look too closely into parked cars. The Saturday night people had an urgent need for and vulnerability to sex, as though the hazy-lighted, dusty, bug-filled air they breathed was a potent aphrodisiac.

Mama always brought the children to the store on Saturday nights. My older sister, who was twelve, grumbled about "getting all dressed up just to stand around in the store." She and her sister had no place else to go and they knew it. Boys were different. Even young ones could wander up and down the streets on Saturday night. Go all the way to Kress's or Woolworth's, even. Nobody paid any attention to boys.

On this Saturday night, Mama and the girls were playing games with the baskets. Mama would send ridiculous items up to the summit where my sisters were. The girls would squeal when they discovered men's long-handled underwear or babies' diapers or ear muffs. I was wearing my best knickers and a flashy striped silk sport shirt I had received a week earlier as a present for my seventh birthday. For a long time I looked outside at Papa who liked to stand on the curb in front of his store on Saturday nights soaking in the reckless, restless mood of the crowd. From time to time Mama would leave the basket game long enough to take a broom and sweep aside some of the dust and trash that drifted into the store. She knew there was no point in closing the door. Papa would reopen it. Papa was a great one for leaving the front door open whenever possible. "Customers are more apt to walk into a store when the door is open," he insisted. His salespeople almost froze in the wintertime.

And then I heard the boom-boom-boom of Old Fats's drum a half-dozen blocks away. The noise of that drum brought with it all the excitement of the streets outside. I ran to Mama and begged, "Let me watch the Army march up Dewey Avenue."

Mama hesitated, then cautioned, "Don't run!"

Papa was so busy talking to his fullblood Indian friend, Wassie Guineahen, he didn't see me dart out of the store and lose myself in the sidewalk crowds. By the time I had reached the corner I could hear the familiar "Onward, Christian Soldiers" and I knew that Major Miller was leading the way up Dewey Avenue with his regulars playing and singing behind him. It wasn't easy squeezing my way around and through the people but I finally met up with the Army on the corner by Kress's. Some of the shoppers in the brightly lighted five-and-dime came out onto the sidewalk to see the marchers and a few waved and smiled at them. Others purposely turned their backs.

Saturday night was hazardous for Major Miller and his crew. While audiences were larger then and donations more generous, heavy traffic forced them to the side of the street and the threat of being sideswiped kept them from concentrating on their music. Corporal Mary Wade used her cymbals as weapons against cars that passed too closely and Steve had to walk gingerly to keep from assaulting bystanders with his trombone flourishes. Captain Bledsoe drooled and spit into his recalcitrant cornet and Old Fats whacked his drum with such zest that one had the feeling he could pummel the head of anybody who got fresh with his fellow marchers and still not miss a beat.

I followed alongside them, sometimes on the curb, sometimes on the street, depending on how hard the crowd pushed me. When they finally reached their reserved place on Main Street just off Dewey Avenue they were obviously relieved.

The Army members had not yet formed their traditional semicircle facing the sidewalk when I heard a woman near me gasp in pain and whine, "Let me go, Eddy."

I looked up and saw a pale and frightened Teresa, her Salvation Army bonnet on the street. She was trying to squirm away from a thick behemoth of an Indian who held her wrists in his hands and was pulling her to him until her face was almost a part of his.

"Eddy! You're hurting me! Let me go!"

"You like it, Teresa. You know you like it. You're gonna come with me. Right now. You know where we're goin' and what we're gonna do."

Someone moved quickly by me and then I heard Major Miller's voice say, "Duck, Teresa." No sooner had she done so than he swung his fist into Eddy's chin with such force that Eddy fell all the way back against the rough red bricks of the City Drug.

Before Eddy could regain his balance Major Miller grabbed him under the collar and growled in a tough-sounding voice I had never heard him use before, "Leave her alone, Eddy. Get it? Leave Teresa alone or . . . I'll kill you."

Eddy just stood there as Major Miller turned his back on him and led Teresa through the crowd that was unaware of any disturbance. Teresa, still trembling, was rubbing her wrists, but she nodded at the others that she was all right, put on her bonnet which Corporal Wade had dusted and smoothed and took her tambourine from Mrs. Miller.

"My friends, Jesus welcomes you!" Major Miller began shakily. "Jesus is with us here tonight . . . right here on this street corner in Sapulpa, Oklahoma!" The heat of the night and his recent exertion made the perspiration roll from under his cap down his face and onto his heavy wool uniform. The bright red Salvation Army band above the brim of his cap was a dark maroon where it had been sweated through. But he kept on speaking to the crowd, urging people to step up closer so they could hear better. "Jesus says, 'God hath anointed Me to preach the gospel to the poor . . . He hath sent Me to heal the brokenhearted.'" Major Miller was not shaky now. "Are *you* in trouble? Let Jesus save you!" He opened his *Salvation Army Song Book* and began to sing,

> "O Lord I will delight in Thee
> And on Thy Care depend . . .
> To Thee in every trouble face,
> My best, my only Friend."

The others held their instruments and sang with him. Beautiful Teresa, almost over her fright now, looked only at the face of Major Miller as she sang. Old Fats carefully turned over his bass drum and pushed it close to the side-walk so that it was in the middle of the Army semicircle. People began to step out of the crowd and drop their offerings on the drum and in a few minutes there was a good deal of change and some dollar bills. I had two dimes in my pocket and walked up to the drum and dropped them onto it. The dimes skidded over the other money and landed against the drum edge, directly in front of Steve. I looked fleetingly at Steve and wondered if I had tempted him by placing his Saturday night quota liter-ally under his nose.

As I stepped backward into the crowd again I landed on a woman's toe. "My corn!" she groaned. Instead of saying I was sorry I tried to escape, ducking between people's legs until I was on the outside of the ring looking up at the backs of the listeners. I had moved so fast that no one could have expected me to be standing where I was. I say that because I can't believe anyone would have spit on me on purpose. But that is precisely what happened in the rhythm of my movements to the wrong spot at the wrong instant. A huge, khaki-clad, oil-field roustabout had turned his head away from the crowd and, aiming for the space between curb and street, had uncorked what seemed to be a full pint of warm tobacco juice. It caught me on the right shoulder and dribbled down the front and back of my silk shirt, adding brown polka-dot splotches to the fancy stripes.

I was overwhelmingly ashamed of myself for something that really was not my fault. I would have run away in fright and disgrace but the spitter saw me and stopped me with a snarled, "Hey!"

He knew who I was, probably from seeing me in Papa's store, and his own guilt at what he'd done, coupled with his earlier visits to the Red Man Bar, brought forth an expletive instead of an apology.

"Jew baby!" he sneered. "Get the hell out of here!"

Jew baby!

I began to cry uncontrollably. Tears of humiliation. I turned my back on the service and was just starting to walk to the store (and more disgrace) when I felt a hand on the shoulder that was wet from its recent drenching. I stopped, and, still crying, slowly turned around to see who was restraining me. Bending over me was Major Miller. He must have had his eye on me all the while and he had seen and heard what had happened.

He squatted down so that his face was on a level with mine and he unfolded his clean white handkerchief and wiped first my eyes and nose—and then my shirt.

"We're going to sing a song you like," he said. "Come and stand by me and sing 'O Boundless Salvation' with us."

He took me by the hand and led me into the semicircle of the Salvation Army. I stood next to Major Miller in the center of the cluster. Mrs. Miller had finished the first verse and I joined the others in the second:

"My sins they are many, their stains are so deep,
And bitter the tears of remorse that I weep;
But useless is weeping, thou great crimson sea,
Thy waters can cleanse me, come, roll over me!"

Major Miller held up his hand. "We'll finish this beautiful hymn in just a minute," he said. "But first let me talk to you about your sins. All of us are sinners. All of us need to be cleansed. . . ."

73

As he preached I found myself studying the faces of the
people in front of us. There weren't many left—a woman
with a baby in her arms, a man in overalls standing quietly
with his wife and two children, a middle-aged woman who
was crying, a drunk, a few more. The man who had bothered
Teresa was gone, and so was the khaki man who had spit on
me and called me that name.

Major Miller continued to preach and as he did so his
audience dwindled and drifted away. The stores were already
closed and people were in a hurry to get home. Saturday
night was almost over.

"Hallelujah!" said Major Miller. "Join us in the last verse
of our song:

> "And now, Hallelujah! The rest of my days
> Shall gladly be spent in promoting His praise. . . ."

As we sang I saw Mama coming toward us. She was
looking for me and was worried when she didn't see me
among the few onlookers. She was about to proceed down
Dewey Avenue when the woman with the baby tapped
Mama on the shoulder and pointed to me.

I had been too busy singing to get Mama's attention but
was delighted that she had seen me now. I waved at her
happily as the Salvation Army and I concluded the song:

> "Who opened His bosom to pour out this sea
> Of boundless salvation for you and for me."

It was Corporal Mary Wade who said to Mama, "Come
and join us, Sister Annie. We'll sing the last chorus again."

"Oh, I don't think I'd better. . . ." Mama started to say,

but when she looked at her friends smiling and beckoning to her . . . the Millers, Teresa, Old Fats, Captain Bledsoe and poor temptable Steve . . . she couldn't resist the impulse to join them.

"And now Hallelujah!" they began again as Mama stepped between Corporal Wade and me and sang with us.

I remember how proud I was of Mama. Maybe she was small in size but from her there came strength and power and love. I often think of Mama at that moment and how beautiful she was. Her Texas upbringing showed itself as she sang the words "the rest of mah days."

I saw Papa before Mama did. He was sitting at the wheel of our Packard which was parked in the middle of the street. My sisters and brother were gawking at us from the back seat but Papa acted like he was someplace else. Suddenly he turned around and handed something to my sister Bea who got out of the car and came over to our group where she placed a dollar bill on the drum.

Mama was in such a hurry to get into the car that Bea and I could hardly keep up with her. Papa, still in a state of shock, started the motor and as we proceeded down Main Street Mama and I turned and waved good-bye to our friends.

"Max," Mama said evenly, "before you explode let me remind you that *your* friends burned a hole in my rug and *your* friends broke my cut-glass lamp." She said no more.

Papa continued to look straight ahead. I hoped Major Miller didn't see him spit just before we turned the corner for home.

3. Mama Herself

Whenever I slide between clean sheets . . . wherever I may be . . . I think first of Mama, then of the President of the United States. Sometimes the memory is so fleeting that it comes and goes before I am fully conscious of it. Other times, the fresh-bed stimulus inspires a whopping mother response and I remember everything from Mama's laugh to her boardinghouse hash to the way she handled my father when he had a temper fit, an ant subduing an elephant.

I'll get to the President in a minute, but first let me say that these fresh-sheet memories have nothing to do with psychology. Even though they are bed triggered they do not indicate dark (not even light gray) oedipal roots. As one of four children I felt sufficiently loved, but not overloved. I received a properly generous amount of loving for the third child in a series of four. My mother feelings shouldn't bring a flicker of suspicion from either Freud or Portnoy. Mine was an uncomplicated, happy childhood (and I sure as hell was never jealous of my father!).

Besides, it isn't the bed that brings back Mama. The sheets do the trick. Whenever one of us kids helped Mama make a bed we knew she'd say, "I wonder if the President of the United States gets clean sheets and pillowcases every single day?" She worried about things like that.

"Your grandmother Lena back in Texas changed the beds twice a week," she said, "and so do I. But I'll bet the President gets everything clean every single day—like in a hotel."

Then she'd argue with herself in that soft Texas drawl she never surrendered to Oklahoma, "Sometimes fresh sheets are scratchy. I knew a woman who starched her sheets. Isn't that awful? I personally feel it's all right to sleep in a bed with the same sheets on it for three or four days. Makes fresh sheets a kind of special treat." Then she'd ask earnestly, "What do you think? Does the President always get clean sheets? I'll bet he does. And I'll bet he gets tired of it. . . ."

When Mama talked like that she made me feel lucky to get to sleep on previously used bedding, and I did feel sorry for the poor President who yearned in vain for just one night on yesterday's sheets.

Lots of things about being President bothered Mama and she wondered about them. Does the President eat every meal, even breakfast, from a clean, pressed tablecloth? ("I could understand using a fresh cloth for breakfast if there were stains or spills on the old one but if it looked perfectly clean, why—") Does the President ever wear the same pair of socks two days in a row? ("Sometimes when the weather's damp things just won't get dry!") Does the President have to give up a comfortable pair of shoes just because they need half soling? And the question that bugged her most: Does the President *ever* eat leftovers?

The thought of never being served leftovers dissipated any

childhood dream I had of being elected President. Imagine missing out on Mama's stuffed green peppers, or meat loaf or hash!

"What's in this wonderful hash?" we'd ask as we helped ourselves to seconds and thirds.

Mama, who had been weaned on Shakespeare in her father's opera house above his store, could quote the Bard without sounding hifalutin' and she borrowed from *Macbeth* for her answer: "Eye of newt and toe of frog, wool of bat and tongue of dog." Then she'd wink and add, "Plus a pinch of chili powder."

People don't make hash like that any more. Some contemporary near misses are labeled stews or ragouts but they don't have the consistency of Mama's hash, which was loose but not runny, and its flavor hot but not spicy.

Mama had the knack of making food taste even more delicious the second time around. When asked how she did it she just shrugged and said, "There's no secret. Anybody can throw things together for a redo." Her stuffed green peppers, reborn from the remains of a leftover roast, reached a higher level of incarnation than in their previous existence. Meat loaf was juicy, chewy, better than steak. Salmon croquettes were round and plump (never shaped like skinny, peaked triangles the way cafeterias serve them), crusty on the outside but soft and moist within. I have spent a lifetime ordering salmon croquettes in restaurants hoping, hoping . . . but when they are served they are too often greasy, hard and overcooked all the way through.

Mama could take bread rejects and by some mysterious alchemy involving raisins, nutmeg and milk (or was it heavy cream?) turn them into a bread pudding so heavenly light you'd study it lovingly (and maybe whisper sweet nothings to it) between bites. Mama never had to encourage us to eat leftovers. Her only problem was to strike a balance between quantities and appetites so there would never have to be a redo of the redo.

If I saw a churn in a kitchen of today I'd do a double take, yet when the too-much milk from Papa's too-many cows turned too sour too fast Mama dumped it into the churn, and guess who churned away until the butter came? I really didn't mind churning. I'd count the plunges. Par for the course was seven hundred strokes. People are able to complete so few of the everyday projects they take on—at least without obstacles, worries and postponements. Churning is different. If you chug right along you'll win every time. What was once merely clabbered milk suddenly becomes delicious buttermilk, with a crown of golden butter on top! Isn't that wonderful? Mama made her own cottage cheese (she tied it in a cheesecloth bag and hung it from the faucet over the kitchen sink so it could drip peacefully), pickled her own tongue, corned her own beef, aged her own fruitcakes.

Great cooks are born, not made. They know instinctively how to produce light-as-a-feather pastry, how to stuff a turkey, how to dream up a mouth-watering casserole. Mama was one of these. She performed her culinary miracles three times a day every day—and without the help of any cookbook.

In the keen competition of cookery that existed in the small town of fifty years ago Mama was an acknowledged champ. Every one in Sapulpa knew that Mrs. Max Meyer had a magic touch with food. She cooked by feel. A pinch of this, a dip of that, a little more sweetenin', a little less thickenin'— it sounds mystical to the modern chef and perhaps it was. Mama communed with her ingredients. She knew when to put things in the oven and when to take them out. Her biscuits were always light and fluffy, her custards always smooth, her fried chicken crisp and greaseless. She wandered in and out of the kitchen while things were cooking, gave a hurried poke or a mechanical baste, then went back to other tasks. She didn't believe in hovering over dishes ("They deserve their own privacy" was the way she put it), yet she never let her corn bread get overbrown, or her baked chicken get too dry or her dumplings get too heavy. She must have possessed a whole tuning band of wave lengths for receiving progress reports because she knew the precise timing for every recipe. I've heard housewives complain about spending hours in the preparation of a meal only to see it devoured in a matter of minutes. Not Mama. If her cooking was attacked with gusto and promptly dispatched that was all she asked.

Specialties?

Mama cooked Texas style but she also made potato pancakes that couldn't emanate from a town named Sapulpa in Oklahoma, but did. Spaghetti? Mama knew how. New England boiled dinner? Baked beans? Stuffed eggplant? Oyster stew? *How!* She served chop suey from a huge rose medallion bowl she'd bought from one of her front-door peddlers.

While she didn't know how to pray the simplest prayer in Hebrew she could cook Jewish dishes that would inspire a rabbi to chant a prayer of Thanksgiving: gefültte fish (served hot for supper or cold with its own jelled sauce, a breakfast delicacy Papa adored), potato latkes, carrot tzimmes, knaidlach balls, stuffed derma, appled strudel.

Some cooks make "A" on soufflés and flunk hamburgers. Mama's true genius came out in the way she could change pace from fancy foods to common dishes. "Who wants fancy cooking all the time?" she said, "even a king likes a hamburger now and then!" Her hamburgers (served on buns with her own piccalilli and her own sweet-and-sour pickles), her chili (it had carne in it but we didn't call it chili con carne; we just called it chili), her flapjacks—she was always chief cook at the annual Salvation Army Pancake Day Benefit—were delicious. Evoking their flavor and taste fifty years later doesn't diminish them a bit.

How lucky Papa was to have married a woman who never complained when he announced that he'd invited five (or ten . . . or twenty) distant cousins he'd met down at the lake for whatever meal was coming up next! In the summertime we ate on the screened-in back porch of the ranch house, which was located just off the kitchen. Long wooden tables, joined together, stretched at least thirty feet, and the benches on either side made it easy to seat thirty people, fifty or sixty in a pinch. Somehow the meat-market-sized icebox always had enough chickens to fry, enough tomatoes to slice, enough just-picked green beans, enough fresh peach ice cream batter to turn.

When my sisters grew older they sometimes became indignant at Papa's spontaneous hospitality, but Mama was the one to protest and she never did. I did. I helped wash the dishes and I came to detest big, fat cousins who had to drive home as soon as they had stuffed themselves, leaving mountains of dishes behind. I begged Mama to use paper plates and paper cups but she wouldn't do it. I realize now that anyone with her respect for good food felt that it deserved decent plates, cutlery and glasses. She occasionally conceded a point on paper napkins but that's as far as she would go.

Mama had an overwhelming passion for preserving. She referred to it as "putting up" things. Every canning season she "put up" enough for an army. Papa, being an extensive (as opposed to intensive) farmer, grew fifty times more than he needed of everything he planted. He would bring home bushel baskets full of peaches, grapes, plums, green beans, tomatoes—even onions!—from his own orchards and gardens. There wasn't much of a market for produce in normal times and during the Depression the market was non-existent. I remember picking perfect Elberta, freestone and cling peaches until my arms ached and sitting all day by Highway 66 near a sign reading PEACHES 75¢ per bushel, only to mark through the 75¢ and change it to 50¢ the next day.

The Depression was a time of contradictions for a good many Oklahomans who, like Papa, would have gone bust with the rest of the nation had it not been for lucky harvests reaped from crops of oil wells others planted for them. Our own Depression came a few years later, after the nation had begun its recovery. When the oil played out our luck played out with it.

The more fruits and vegetables Papa brought in, the greater the challenge to Mama. I've seen the time when Beulah and Beulah's Sister and Beulah's Sister's sister-in-law were peeling peaches without letup while Mama darted about the kitchen like a woman possessed, making batches of peach preserves and peach butter. (The butter was another utilization of leftovers. It was made from the "leavings." Because it was more sour than sweet I liked it even better than the richer preserves.)

Where are the jars of yesteryear? Where have they gone . . . the hundreds and hundreds of glass containers Mama bought for preserving and canning? Mason jars were the best known, but there were Ball jars, Kerr jars, and Premium jars. Ball Brothers fruit jars were made in Sapulpa at the Schram Glass Factory. These Ball jars had lead tops with glass fillers and Mama liked them as well as she did Mason jars. But her favorite for peaches, pears, pickles and canned whole fruits or vegetables was the Premium, a wide-mouthed jar with a flat glass top. The Premium jar was made at Sapulpa's Liberty Glass Company and it had a kind of metal fastener made of galvanized wire which went onto the jar like a bicycle clamp. First you'd put a rubber band on your glass jar filled with something showy like pickled peaches, then you'd fit the glass top on, then you'd put on the clasp and turn it as you would a lid to seal in the contents. As common as Premium jars were then, they are rare and costly antiques today.

I can still see Mama at canning time: every inch of table or cabinet space in the huge kitchen and the adjoining dining porch of the Oak Street house was taken up with rows and rows of sterilized jars, their mouths open, waiting to be filled. Mama would put a sterling knife into each jar to keep it from breaking when she poured the hot contents into it. The tops were never tightened until the jars were cool. Then she'd prevail upon Papa to give each jar a nice strong turn to seal it tight. Jellies and strawberry preserves (one year Papa planted five acres of strawberries just to see if they'd grow in Oklahoma; they grew) were administered paraffin toppings. Paraffin was supposed to seal them and keep them fresh and I guess it did, but I hated wrestling with the opaque stuff whenever it was time to get into a jar. Instead of slipping up neatly when pressure was applied to the rim the paraffin too often cracked and crumbled and had to be fished out of its gooey sea with fingers.

One room of the basement of the house on Oak Street—
the one adjoining the ironing room—was walled with shelves.
These shelves were always solidly lined with Mama's canned
goods. In another part of the basement, down a passageway
too dark for children to explore, Mama operated her own
winery. It was a strange thing, the wine making. Everybody
seemed to take a personal interest in its progress, yet it was
always discussed in whispers.

Of course our family could never consume all the food
Mama put up, and over the years Major Miller at the Salvation Army gratefully received hundreds of those filled Mason,
Premium, Ball and Kerr jars. But since Mama never fussed
at Papa for his wanton planting Papa never complained to
her about her kitchen excesses.

Women don't put up fruits and vegetables the way they
used to. We live in the Freezer Age and maybe that's
good, but Mama wouldn't like the new way of freezing
things. She got her kicks from marching up and down in
front of the rows of jars, all filled and sealed and wiped to a
shine, admiring the color of the plum jelly, the consistency
of the peach butter, the beauty of the pickles, the plump-
ness of the strawberries, the glory of it all.

In Mama's book, food was the answer to any problem,
balm for any hurt. I sometimes think that my father could
have beaten her black and blue and still kept her love—so
long as he asked for more noodle soup, more dressing, more
blackberry cobbler. Mama believed that people who ate
heartily were happier. People who picked at their food had
to be sick. When trouble came to friends or neighbors Mama
cooked the dinner and sent it over. When babies were born

85

at home (and most of them were), Mama would stick her head into the new mother's room and say reassuringly, "Don't worry, honey. I brought a little something for everybody to eat," then leave it and run.

As each one of her four children left home for college Mama sent that child food packages twice a month until graduation. It was Mama's way of making us feel loved, missed . . . and nourished! She knew how to pack food so it would defy time and distance and keep perfectly. During my years at Dartmouth College Mama sent food boxes regularly, all the way from Sapulpa, Oklahoma, to Hanover, New Hampshire—to my own delight and to the delight of my roommates and friends. There was always plenty: a baked chicken or turkey or goose, with one pint jar filled with dressing, another with cranberry sauce, another with cooked apples, another with her incomparable potato salad. There was always a chocolate cake or cupcakes or both. Then for three years of law school at Ann Arbor, Michigan, it was more of the same. Maybe Mama had in mind more than just a gift of food for her children. Maybe she wanted to ensure our popularity. For the seven years that those food boxes came I was neither hungry nor friendless!

Food was a kind of blessing with Mama, a way of life. Some people sing, some play the piano, some dance. Mama cooked. All she asked was an appreciative audience. Second helpings were her encores.

Once upon a time there were no antibiotics. Nor were there tranquilizers, pep pills, or even one-a-day vitamin capsules. There were only home remedies.

Part of the success of home remedies was the absolute

belief in their efficacy by the person who practiced them. *Take bumps.* Mama had an odd sort of first aid for bumps on the head. She would take a table knife and press it against the rising bump until she was satisfied she'd stopped the swelling. I've never heard of anyone before or since who tried that one, but I'm sure she didn't make it up.

Take regurgitation. Mama used to say, "A child is at his most helpless when he has to throw up." She just couldn't stand by while her children were being sick at their stomachs. She felt needed at that awful moment when dignity is lost and the law of gravity suspended. So when one of us raced for the bathroom to be sick Mama raced right in behind him and always held his or her head tightly between her hands, one palm pressing hard against the child's forehead, the other pressing hard against the back of the head. It was a very great comfort to the helpless child, both physically and emotionally, but how Mama struggled through the ordeal without getting sick herself is a mystery. I tried it once with one of my own children and I got sicker than she did.

The first time Papa saw Mama assisting one of us this way in the moment of need he yelled at Mama from the hall into the bathroom, "What in the hell are you doing?" It made him nervous whenever our bodies didn't behave as he thought they should, so he'd stand by at a safe distance and hide his bewilderment by swearing loudly at Mama.

"I'm making it easier for this child," Mama replied impatiently, holding the young head fore and aft, tensing for the next wave. "Go *'way,* Max. Just *go 'way!*"

"Easier?" Papa roared. "What do you mean easier? Can't that kid aim himself without you having to aim him?"

"I'll give you five seconds to close that bathroom door, Max!" Mama threatened grimly, still holding the head tightly. "And don't you *dare* . . ."

He slammed the door viciously.

"Slam it."

Not only remedies have changed. Diseases have, too. What, for example, has happened to the croup? You never hear that word any more, yet Mama was constantly talking about croup—and taking steps to counteract it. If we had the faintest suggestion of a congestion Mama started putting up barricades against the croup. Her principal ally was goose grease. She always kept a jar in the back of the icebox for emergencies. If Mama decided that the croup was imminent, then before going to bed at night we had to submit to hot goose grease being rubbed onto our chests with flannel cloths for buffers. Next morning we went to school with the flannel cloths (thoroughly saturated and horribly greasy) pinned to our underwear. Goose grease (the original *schmaltz*) is great for cooking purposes, but when worn near, under or around the armpits for a couple of days it is worse than tear gas in its effects on other people. Of course the goose-grease-on-flannel-cloth remedy works. Those who wear the cloths don't catch croup—or anything else. They smell so high other people stay at a considerable distance. It is axiomatic that if you don't come into close contact with others you won't catch their germs!

When it came to cure-alls, Mama and Papa had two basic disagreements: He was convinced that he could save the world with Mentholatum and Epsom salts. Mama was just as positive that if the world was to be saved it would have to be through Camphophenique and castor oil.

Papa bought Mentholatum in the large economy sizes. I can still hear him say to us children at bedtime, "Stuff a little Mentholatum up your nose. Even if you don't need it, it will do you good." Then he'd exhort, "More, more! *Inhale* like good soldiers!" We inhaled like good soldiers but we stored away Mentholatum resentments future psychiatrists would glory in.

If Mama heard about a sore throat before Papa did she started warming her goose grease and getting the flannel ready. If Papa got the draw he raced for the Mentholatum, buttered a cloth thickly and then pinned it around the ailing child's throat. The first cloth won. I'm sure Mama was tempted more than once to remove the Mentholatum collar and substitute in its place a schmaltzy one but she didn't dare do it.

If you are jaded, if you've tried everything from pot to paint thinner and are still searching for a new and different sensation, I recommend Papa's Mentholatum collar! The ice cold shock from the initial contact gives way to dozens of subsequent clammy shocks as the loose cloth flops against the neck. It is a truly unique feel sensation. Indescribable.

When we children were not smeared and greased like Channel swimmers by Papa (the official Mentholatum season ran from October to April), we reeked of Mama's aromatic Camphophenique. How our teachers stood us is the real miracle.

Camphophenique has an aroma all its own. Even if you like the smell of camphor, the phenique part will sneak up from behind and cut you down. Camphophenique was Mama's miracle antiseptic. She used it for cuts, burns, bruises, bumps, itching feet and (I hesitate saying this but I must for the record) for hemorrhoids. She may even have used it as a mouthwash or for other hygienic purposes for all I knew.

The battle lines were really drawn on the issue of purges. To Papa, there was only one: Epsom salts. To Mama there was only one: castor oil. Each was convinced that his was the only proper palliative. They engaged in a violent competition for patients and each had his own intricate secret service system involving bribes for tips that might lead to incipient sniffles or stomach-aches. The one who "got there first" got to use his favorite medicine. We children were strictly neutral. We surrendered only when caught because we disliked one purge as much as we did the other.

Papa prescribed Epsom salts externally as a foot bath, in packs for toothache and rheumatism, as a solution to soak infections in. But it was as an internal panacea that he valued the bitter liquid most. He boasted of his famous "course" which consisted of a light (!) dose of salts every morning for seven days. What his course did to me and to everyone who took it is something I discussed in depth in the book I wrote about him. Papa's Epsom obsession is documented. Now it is Mama's turn.

Mama made a few external passes with her castor oil—it was great for removing warts, for loosening soft corns, for baby's chafing—but she, too, was internally oriented. You had to swallow it to get the full benefit. One advantage of Mama's oil over Papa's salts was that one dose did it all. There was no "course." If you could get the glassful of oil down (and keep it down) you were sure to feel better.

To compound the torture, Mama always added to the four ounces (more or less, usually more) of castor oil the juice of two oranges. She had the grace to strain the juice first but even so an occasional seed would secrete itself in the mixture. One of the worst things that can happen to a human being is to be swallowing castor oil as rapidly as you can and come upon a seed suspended there. You can't stop and spit it out. You can't tuck it back in your mouth to be spit out later. You just have to go ahead and swallow the damned thing and hope the oil will take care of it.

But wait! Mama had still another ingredient to add to the dose. She poured a bit of whiskey on top of the orange juice.

I remember being sick once on the day Mama entertained her Shakespeare Club. Mrs. Simpson happened to come into the kitchen as Mama was putting the finishing touches on my dose of castor oil (which she invariably served in a cut-glass water tumbler).

"Why in the world do you put that whiskey in it?" she asked Mama.

"It cuts the taste of the oil," Mama said. And then she added sagely, "He'll never like the taste of whiskey because it will always make him think of castor oil!"

Mama meant well but she had her signals mixed. Despite her clever attempt at conditioning me against whiskey I got so I liked the taste of the stuff very much indeed. Too much, in fact.

But to this day I can't stand orange juice.

Mama liked simple but expressive nicknames. We always had a dog and he was always called Junior. If he was a she then she was called Junior. Junior meant dog to us from the moment we learned to speak. Most of our Juniors were hounds but at various times we had a collie Junior, an airedale Junior and a bird dog Junior.

We always used the word "blinky" for "sleepy." I don't know where Mama found that one but I still catch myself saying, "I'm blinky," when it's time for bed. Mama got me started calling my two sisters Little Sister and Big Sister. I continued addressing them by those names until I was in law school, at which time my sisters prevailed upon me to call them by their given names. It wasn't easy to change the habit. My brother was called Baby until he was a major in the army. Papa called me Sonny Boy, Mama called me Sonny, and my sisters referred to me as Son. (If the terms Big Sister and Little Sister caused raised eyebrows you can imagine the reaction to a grown woman absent-mindedly calling a grown man "Son" in public!)

At the risk of being indelicate I must reveal Mama's words for children's bodily functions. When it came to frontal maneuvers she refused to settle for wee-wee or tinkle; she preferred that we say (I am embarrassed about this but I'm started so I'll continue) "bow wow." Strangers were constantly perplexed at hearing Mama's children, from tiny to middlin', announce loudly that they had to "go bow wow." Once or twice playful adults who thought it was some sort of childish game tried bow wowing back at us. Mama tried to explain to them why these were urgent communications but she never had the time to do so because when you've got to bow wow you've got to bow wow.

Mama really had a lulu for the other announcement. It took real ingenuity to come up with the word "prettyway." It was all one, unhyphenated, run-together word: prettyway. When one of her children declared that he had to make prettyway Mama went into action. I always meant to ask Mama through what etymological hocus-pocus she had hit upon that particular word for that particular act. *Prettyway*, indeed!—a nine-letter word I've never seen scrawled anywhere. Graffiti collectors—it's yours!

Fortunately for us, Mama wasn't superstitious. Papa was constantly spitting, touching wood and crossing fingers. Mama blamed it on his Arkansas heritage. "He's got all the Ozark superstitions," she said, "plus a hundred more." He respected the routine superstitions like broken mirrors, side-stepping stepladders, avoiding the number thirteen, throwing spilled salt over the left shoulder, and knocking wood. He also forbade anyone to walk around with one shoe on and one shoe off, to whistle in the house (you could sing all you pleased, but you dassn't whistle), or put a hat on a bed. If someone sewed a button on a shirt you were wearing you had to chew a piece of thread while the sewing was going on. Papa gave black cats a wide berth. Once, on our way to Tulsa in the family car, a black cat ran across the road. Papa slammed on the brakes and refused to continue until each person in the car, including Mama, had spit seven times. (I have wondered since if that is where the expression "scared spitless" originated?)

It was a constant challenge living with Papa's superstitions, his temper, his Mentholatum and his Epsom salts—but Mama had other crosses to bear, many of which she kept to herself. I was in my thirties when Papa confided one of them to me.

My first child was about to be born. Papa and I were the only two people in the dimly lit hospital waiting room for expectant fathers. It was four in the morning when the doctor announced to us that I had a daughter, Papa had a granddaughter, and that the mother was doing fine.

"You were acid, just like me," Papa said. That is, I *thought* that was what he said but it made no sense so I ignored it.

"Well!" I exulted. "A baby girl! One of her names is going to be Ann—after Mama."

Papa reacted as he always did when Mama was mentioned. He turned his head and blinked his eyes and swallowed hard. Almost ten years had gone by since she'd left us, yet her buoyancy and bounce were still a part of all our lives. We missed her, especially at milestone times like this.

"Sonny Boy," he confided, "there's something I've never told you."

That was an odd thing to say at four A.M. while we were unwinding from the tension of our vigil. "You mean . . . now that I'm a father I'm old enough to hear it?" I asked.

"Now that you're the father of a *girl*," he answered. "My first one was a girl, too, so I understand your disappointment."

"But I'm not disappointed!" I said almost belligerently. "We *wanted* a girl. I *like* little girls."

"Impossible," Papa answered stubbornly. "You've got to have sons. Boys keep the name alive. The Bible talks about Abraham, Isaac and Jacob. Not Annie, Ida or Jennie. Don't worry, though. I'll tell you how to have a boy for sure next time. You've got to be alkaline at the moment you . . . conceive." It took a big effort for Papa to get that last word out. Even though I had proved I knew the facts of life he didn't like to discuss them with me.

"There's nothing anybody can do to influence the sex of an unborn child," I argued. "You go right on rooting for Abrahams. I'll take Annies every time!"

"That's what your mother said forty years ago," Papa replied. "She didn't believe me when I told her there was a . . . a way."

"Way?"

"Yes. It's a scientific principle but it's hushed up because it wouldn't be right if everybody knew about it."

"About what?" I was too tired to move so I egged Papa on.

"Well, if the man is alkaline at the moment of conception his offspring will be a boy. If his body is acid at that moment he'll father a girl. It's a fact. I was overacid the first two times but then I worked it a little more careful-like and got you and your brother."

"Tell me more," I said, sensing that if Papa didn't continue this story now he probably never would.

"It was a hot day in June. *Real* hot. Your mama and I lived in a dusty little rent house on Cedar Street, the one I bought later on and moved to the other end of Dewey Avenue. I'd already started building the house on Oak Street and I was allowing plenty of room for expansion." He stopped for a moment thinking of something and then he blurted out, "It was a *Sunday!* Yes, I'm positive it was a Sunday because when Annie sent me out for some fresh air I remember everything was closed. It was one helluva hot Sunday in June and I drank bicarbonate of soda until I was sick as a horse and your mother thought I was crazy."

I could see it so plainly. All those years ago, long before I was born: just Papa and Mama in a frame house on a broiling hot Sunday. Mama, unused to brash and pushy Oklahoma, Indian Territory, a stranger still to housekeeping—and to marriage—homesick for Taro where the living was easy, dressed in a white voile long-sleeved dress because that's what she would have worn at home on Sunday, her waist so tiny Papa could cup it between his two hands. And there was Papa: drinking glass after glass of water with baking soda in it, and getting sicker and sicker.

"That was the whole trouble," Papa continued. "A *little* bicarb keeps you alkaline but too much *over*alkalizes you and turns you acid. I didn't know it then. I kept on drinking that terrible, bitter stuff and I began to burp so bad I

95

thought I'd explode. That's when Annie sent me out for a walk. I had to get relief. Gas embarrasses me."

I nodded. Papa had gas. Neither Mama's castor oil nor his own Epsom salts had any effect on Papa's flatulence. Mama just lived with it, and so did we.

"When I got back from my walk my stomach was still rumbling something fierce but I felt it was time for us to . . . to . . . I mean, I'd gone *that* far so there was no point in calling it quits."

He paused, cornering old memories in that small hospital waiting room. "I'll say one thing for Annie. She was a sport about it. Didn't even bring up the subject when Bea was born."

"Do you think Mama believed it?" I asked.

"Maybe not then—but after you and your brother were born I think she did. Your mother had an open mind about most things."

He yawned. "I've told you all this so's you'll know what to do next time. Stop the bicarb after the first burp and you've got it made."

"Thanks, Papa," I said getting up. "Let's find the doctor and ask him if he'll permit your acid son to see his wife and daughter."

"You don't *have* to be acid . . ." he began.

"But I like little girls," I repeated. "I hope I stay acid forever."

I have.

4. "I've Got a Feelin' You're Foolin'"

People thought it was silly the way we drove back and forth from town to country and then back to town again. It wasn't unusual for Papa to make half a dozen round trips a day. We used to call Papa's preserve of natural stone and prodigious plantings both a ranch and a farm and I find myself still doing it. Was it farm—or was it ranch? Papa always said ranch. The word had a nice expansiveness and it allowed him the added pleasure of picturing himself as a rancher. In the pre-plumbing, pre-electricity years Mama called it a farm and sometimes in later years she would lapse into the old habit and say "farm," but as the conveniences came along she, too, gravitated toward ranch, particularly when Papa was around.

The farm-ranch house was only five miles from the house on Oak Street and many of Mama's friends, including most of the Shakespeare Club, kept telling her to make it easy on herself and settle on one of the two houses for her permanent home. Mrs. Anderson, who loved to illustrate her point with a Shakespearean quote, never failed to remind Mama that her dual housekeeping efforts were "love's labour's lost." The first time I heard her say it I winced and complained, "How corny can you get?" Mama came to Mrs. Anderson's defense with, "Mrs. Anderson is also convinced that a rolling stone gathers no moss and a stitch in time saves nine—but she hasn't missed a single Shakespeare Club meeting in three years!"

Mama conceded that the constant movement from town to country and back again entailed extra labor but she didn't feel that anything was lost. It wasn't too much trouble cooking in town and serving at the ranch, nor laundering sheets in town and sleeping on them in the country. You could get used to almost anything, including packing a car at one place and unpacking it fifteen minutes later someplace else.

On a typical Sunday, Mama, Papa, the four children and Junior, our dog, would pull out of the Oak Street driveway, nestled around a tub of potato salad, a dishpan filled with at least five fried chickens (Mama's fried chicken was disjointed: thighs and drumsticks went their separate ways; breasts, backs and wings were laws unto themselves), jars of pickled beets, cooked peas, spiced peaches, cranberries, homemade rolls, jugs of iced tea (already sugared and lemoned), a three-layer devil's food cake, tablecloths and napkins, silverware, books, magazines, phonograph records (thick Edison ones at first and then thin Brunswicks), games and a fifty-pound chunk of ice.

We'd spot the ranch a full mile away, as soon as we reached the crest of the straightaway on Highway 66. Likely as not, Ernie Cooper would have the flag flying at the top of the 150-foot flagpole. Ernie flew the flag on every conceivable occasion, including Sundays, Yom Kippur, Mother's Day, Labor Day and Groundhog Day. As Papa slowed the car he held out his hand for at least fifty yards. Then he came to a dead stop. Then he'd stick his head out the car window and check traffic from both directions before making his left turn into the drive. The driveway went straight ahead for one hundred feet, then turned right at the flagpole and made a circle around the house. Ultimately, after turning right to reach left, we pulled up under the porte-cochere and began disentangling ourselves.

Invariably, Papa jumped out first, ran around the L-shaped porch, unlocked the front door, tore through the living room and dining room to open the side door, waved an all clear to us, then raced from room to room opening windows to "get some fresh air into this place." He ended his tour with the kitchen windows, then unlocked the kitchen door, strode across the back porch and down the back steps and aimed for the dusty road along which most of his tenant farmers lived, an area known as Max Meyer's WPA Row.

My brother would wriggle out from under the potato salad, open the car door so Junior could jump out of his tight quarters, and then the two of them would each race the other in the direction of the lake. My sisters would spot Ernie Cooper or one of the cowhands at the barn and run there squealing for a couple of horses to be saddled for them. That left Mama and me to carry the provisions into the house. I'd let her take the chicken inside and then I'd insist on toting in the rest of the stuff myself. Mama called it my hairshirt complex. It meant loading my arms, walking up the six high steps to the porch, wrestling the screen door open, depositing the things inside, then going back for more until everything was in. I can still hear the slam of that door behind me—and feel its nip when I didn't move fast enough. I not only felt sorry for myself but I hated every member of the family, including Junior.

Time helped. Papa ran a pipeline from the kitchen to one of the oil wells, and the waste gas enabled us to replace the old wood stove with a gas burner. There was the constant threat that an uneven flow of gas would blow up the place (the person who struck the match bent as far away from the stove as possible and stayed in a sprint position), but Mama was happier because now she could prepare most of the meal where it would be eaten. Electricity meant a Frigidaire and the end of balancing a hunk of ice in one hand while opening that pesky screen door with the other. Papa's meat-market icebox held at least three hundred pounds and the fifty-pound block had always looked ridiculously puny inside it. As soon as school was out for the summer we started sleeping at the farm and eating all our meals there and the only thing that had to be toted back and forth then was Beulah.

I think Mama actually liked this crazy arrangement of living in two houses. The ranch house with its haphazard furnishings, created a free-and-easy atmosphere with a minimum of upkeep. Most of the chairs were of the overstuffed variety, many of them hand-me-downs from the house in town and the Main House in Taro.

In order to achieve a fresh and happy feeling to the ranch house, Mama chose slipcover materials patterned in screaming yellows, bruised blues and floral patterns so vivid it was a pleasure to be able to squelch them by sitting on them.

Only someone who knew Mama well—Uncle Sam, perhaps, or maybe old Emma—could see her fine hand at work in this seemingly miscellaneous collection of heavy pieces. When analyzed, the chairs, couches and tables were all Grand Rapids Indestructible. There wasn't a spindly leg or a fluted arm or a glass top in the whole ranch house. Papa at his angriest couldn't do more than turn over one of the slip-covered chairs, and in order to do that he'd first have to wrestle its wildly patterned biceps. Since nobody smoked, there were no ashtrays to be broken. Papa adored built-in cabinets. There were cabinets on both sides of the fireplace and inside one of these was what looked like a battered tin pie plate. This was brought out whenever a guest was about to burn his fingers from glowing ashes. Nor were there any knickknacks for Papa to seize and throw through the nearest window, no lamps for him to knock over to make a point, no potted plants to unpot. If Mama had retained an interior decorator to design a livable area that would frustrate the most manic Menninger boarding student in his wildest temper fit she couldn't have succeeded better than she did with her seemingly casual interiors.

Her plan worked. Never once did Papa go on a de-structive binge at the farm. He saved his temper for the house in town where Mama kept her nice things, including the precious acquisitions from her irresistible peddlers.

Years later, when Papa was too old to get mad and I was old enough to risk being insolent, I brought up the subject of why he got mad enough to break things only when he was in town. He had his answer. "The fresh air in the country kept me calmed down," he said. Baloney. Mama's early twentieth-century sanitarium décor did the trick!

I suspect now that Mama also liked an arrangement whereby she and Papa always had one house they could retreat to in order to be alone.

"I think I'll drive into town with your father when he takes Beulah home," Mama would say.

"Isn't that nice of your mother to come along and keep me company?" Papa would say pleasantly. "Now it won't be such a boring drive."

Mama would respond with "the pleasure is all mine." If she had anything else in mind she fooled us completely.

To Papa the ranch meant fresh air, exercise and wholesome pursuits. It meant a stiff breeze even on the most sweltering day and being able to boast about "needing a quilt last night while you people in town were burning up."

Mama loved the ranch because it gave her family a togetherness long before that word was ever coined. She knew that after supper we'd wander off in different directions: to the nursery to cut an armload of roses blooming on the unsold bushes, or to the lake for a quick dip, or for a twilight walk up the winding road that climbed to the top of the hill where we could see the lights come on in Tulsa fifteen miles away. But when it got good and dark Mama wanted everybody together and that's the way it was. One or two of the kids pumped the porch swing into a dizzy ride or played games up and down the front stone steps. The rest of us sat on chairs or benches on the sidewalk near the fountain.

The fountain! That's what we called that thing, a fountain, even though it had always been and would always be waterless. In the shadow of the flagpole, Papa had planned a huge circular cement fountain with an inner cement circle which would contain an ornamental spout. Who knows? He might even have envisioned colored lights and goldfish. It looked like the ruins of the structure he had planned but had never completed. There, by this strange, fountainless fountain we'd gather in the evenings and talk and sometimes even sing. The stars above us were so vivid it was like being in a planetarium, and when a star would fall, leaving its tail of white sparks behind it, the lucky person who spied it first would yell, "Money, money, money!" That meant certain riches.

As soon as it got chilly Papa always said, "You girls had better get your mother something to put over her shoulders." That was their cue to go indoors and squeeze some fresh lemonade which they'd serve on a tray with some of Mama's cupcakes. Mama would thank them for the shawl and she never failed to act surprised at the treat.

It all seems dreamlike now, mainly because people don't do things like that any more. They don't sit outdoors and look at the sky and drink lemonade and make wishes on falling stars until they are drugged with drowsiness and contentment. They stay indoors these days, where the air conditioning is, and they stare at the one-eyed wonder of the age, television, until they are stultified, immobile, zombied. And when it's time for bed they are neither drowsy nor contented. They are wakeful, unfulfilled—and bored.

As the years went by the ranch had other uses. It was an ideal place for college chums to come for exchange visits. Easterners who had invited me to their homes during Thanksgiving and Easter recesses came to Oklahoma to spend part of their summer vacations on an honest-to-gosh ranch (maybe it was and maybe it wasn't). There were always two or three young guests around, sometimes more.

Those were golden days in more ways than one. Thirty-one oil wells fulfilled Mama's precognition and Papa's dream.

Some of the by-products of that free-flowing crude oil included riding horses in the barn, a five-acre lake—excavated
according to Papa's blueprint specifications to include a deep
"jump off," a three-tiered diving tower and a sanded beach
—tennis courts built from imported clay, and trails which
led across the highway to the top of our own hill or along the
far side of the lake to the bottom of our own canyon. My
parents encouraged us to share the place with our friends and
we did. Perhaps, without knowing what they were doing at
the time, they taught us what Being Rich was really like.

Being Rich meant owning the luxuries of life which you
shared with your friends. Only sometimes your friends, well-
mannered ones from good families, had a peculiar concept of
sharing. They ran your horses mercilessly up and down WPA
Road, cut across the open pastures, raced up to the top of the
hill and then back to the barn at a sustained and brutal
gallop. They slithered off their saddles and left the winded
horses standing there in their stalls, their hides lathered
white with sweat. Nor did the riders bother to remove the
saddles nor offer so much as a lick of salt or a drink of water
to the exhausted animals. The farm hands swore bitterly at
such inhumanity and it hurt us, too, to see our horses abused
that way.

Being Rich meant forcing yourself to be courteous when a
guest borrowed your best tennis racket and knocked the heck
out of it. Then, because he'd forgotten (or was too lazy) to
change from leather soles to tennis shoes, he kicked up hunks
of clay on the tennis courts Ernie Cooper had spent so
many hours rolling and marking to perfection.

Being Rich meant knowing that your guests would enjoy
their swim in your clear and beautiful lake and then ignore
the bathhouse your father had built for them to change and

shower in. Instead, they'd track their sandy footprints inside and leave a trail of drippings across the shining floors.

Being Rich gave you the feeling that maybe people didn't like you for yourself but only used you for what you owned. It made you cynical and turned you from extrovert to introvert. It made you wish you weren't rich because you didn't like seeing your friends at their worst.

Long before the oil stopped flowing (and it did) I was fed up with Being Rich. I wanted nothing more than to leave Being Rich to others and just to concentrate on Being Happy. There's a difference. Only those who had experienced both can make the proper comparison. As for me, I will sign an affidavit that I am happier driving a nondescript car today than I was driving the Pierce Arrow convertible or the seven-passenger Cadillac (the oil wells were gushing, why not buy the best for the children?) day before yesterday. The horses —all of them—are long since gone with the wind that swept through Oklahoma and I, for one, am relieved to say it. The lake is no longer for swimming, the tennis courts are merely scars upon the lawn, the hiking trails are underbrush. So what?

If it is nice Being Rich it is infinitely nicer not being used. Besides, once you've been rich you've had the feel and power of it. And you've learned how little money has to do with richness.

A farm—or a ranch? Whatever you chose to call it, it turned out to be a valuable proving ground, and I learned a lot from it.

The great cigarette conspiracy could never have been hatched if there had not been a Max Meyer ranch. To a mailing clerk in the distant shipping department of the American Tobacco Company the word "ranch" was all-covering. It obviously meant a wide-open space in Oklahoma where affluent visitors came to rest in the sun or ride horses or sing songs around a campfire. The Oak Street address was out. Any single residence was immediately suspect in the bringing off of such a giant fraud. But a ranch? Perfect! On a ranch there could be dozens of people drawn to a lively Saturday night radio show which offered them a chance to win themselves some free Lucky Strike cigarettes merely by sending in a penny postcard with five song titles on it.

There's never been a contest like that one. It must have cost the Lucky Strike people a fortune in postage and contest expenses alone, not to mention the millions of cigarettes they had to give away week after week. It cost them plenty of headaches, too, because clusters of tricksters just like us from one end of the country to the other kept gumming up the works until the prize situation got hopelessly out of hand. Taking place as it did in the mid-thirties when millions of Depression victims still had time on their hands and no place to go, the contest was a splendid thing because it gave idle people something to do. In a larger sense, it gave hope to people who had lost hope. If you didn't win this week there was still something to look forward to next week: the chance of winning a carton of Luckies if the top songs were in the order you predicted they would be.

The Lucky Strike Hit Parade was a Saturday night institution. Its format was idiot oriented. The Hit Parade orchestra and singers presented the ten leading popular songs of the week (CRASH OF CYMBALS . . . "Scientifically based on sheet music and record sales" . . . CRASH OF CYMBALS . . . "Plus the number of performances on juke boxes from one end of America to the other!" . . . CRASH OF CYMBALS). Then, as the show progressed, the announcer's voice trembled with excitement as he worked up the ladder of hits. We trembled, too, as we waited like predators to see how many cigarettes we had beat the company out of with our mass production forecasting.

A musicologist could argue that while the titles changed it was always the same song. The Hit Parade orchestra had a way of emasculating every melody it played. Fast, slow, hot or sweet, the Hit Paraders reduced it to the same unchanging beat: a wild and racy, one-two, one-two, one-two, oompah, oompah, oompah. From the first bars of the opening theme . . . "LUCK-y days are HERE a-GAIN!" to the sign-off commercial everything played, sung or spoken was neutered. The music was that of a calliope in the center of a merry-go-round—all toots, whistles and steam. This hell-bent-for-election gait didn't affect the up-tempo tunes so much. Lively hits like "I'm Gonna Sit Right Down and Write Myself a Letter" or "I've Got a Feelin' You're Foolin'" sounded all right in their Hit Parade straitjacket. The slow songs were the ones that really suffered. "For Sentimental Reasons" or "Love Thy Neighbor" or "These Foolish Things Remind Me of You" sounded awful in the juiced-up cadence.

The entire Hit Parade sounded as though the principal stockholder of American Tobacco had set his metronome at the fastest possible speed and had commanded the musical director to keep up with the pace or find employment elsewhere. Since professional musicians were jobless along with everybody else it evidently wasn't hard to find a conductor who did as he was told, dutifully plowing "I'm an Old Cowhand," "Don't Blame Me," "Ole Faithful," "The Lady in Red" and "Moonlight and Shadows" into the same furrow.

For years the Hit Parade was a full-hour program.

To pad out the time, several "Lucky Strike extras" were thrown in, but the tempo never varied. "Oh, Promise Me," "a timely tribute to the month of June and to June brides evvvvvvvvvvvvverywhere!," picked right up where "Goody Goody" left off. Years later, after Lucky Strike Green Had Gone to War, the radio show was streamlined to thirty minutes and this shorter version ultimately became a none-too-successful television show. But by then the world had wearied of that unyielding rhythm and the Hit Parade itself was no longer in the Top Five. The summertime conspirators from the Max Meyer ranch had lost interest in the show a long time before that. In fact, as soon as they stopped giving away cartons of cigarettes that oompah beat began to get monotonous.

I could be wrong, but the way I remember it all you had to do was predict the top five tunes in the order of their popularity. There was nothing to buy. Entries had to be in the mail by Tuesday midnight to qualify for the following Saturday night's Hit Parade standings.

Picking the top five hits wasn't as difficult as it might seem. The songs climbed and dropped slowly. During the five weeks that "You Are My Lucky Star" was Number One, "There's a Small Hotel" was always Number Two and "Until the Real Thing Comes Along" was always Number Three. Each of those also-rans, in turn, had its own day as Number One. Barring an unexpected dark horse like "Pennies from Heaven," which zoomed into the top five from nowhere, there were only four or five titles to juggle around each week to make a sure-fire winning guess. If each contestant played according to the rules and sent in only one entry his chance of winning depended on luck and skill.

But who paid attention to the rules? Each of us sent in

no less than twenty entries every week. My all-time high was seventy-three. We made every conceivable type of combination, wheeling four other titles around an almost shoo-in much as a horseplayer does in selecting his daily doubles. This systematic approach pushed the skill quotient up and the luck factor down. The only hard part was thinking up enough names to put on all the entries. One had to beware of using the same name too many times. In

The Max Meyer Ranch

Box 27

Sapulpa, Oklahoma

we had a made-to-order address. All we had to do was populate it from our imaginations and that we did.

Every Saturday night was a veritable Walpurgis there in the ranch living room. The conspirators crowded around the radio and screamed or groaned as the Hit Parade standings built dramatically from Number Five to Number One.

The prizes were worth scheming for. Each correct entry won a ten-pack carton of Lucky Strike cigarettes. Ten packages of cigarettes—*free!* Even to a nonsmoker this was a juicy reward. You could get all kinds of favors from people who did smoke by presenting them with a whole carton of free cigarettes. It gave the winner a nice sense of power to bestow favors on grateful recipients. I felt almost omnipotent the week I won twenty-two cartons of Lucky Strikes by putting most of my eggs in one basket and making "Goody Goody," "I'm an Old Cowhand" and "It's De-Lovely" One, Two and Three for the week, then shuffling three other possibilities around for numbers Four and Five. That was my moment of glory, all right, but as it turned out it was too glorious. My jackpot, coupled with the winning entries of others in our ring, turned out to be the hole in the dike that brought the ultimate flood upon us.

Mama got her first inkling that the children were up to something devious when Mrs. Major Miller cornered her in the Safeway store and thanked her for the cigarettes.

"Cigarettes?" Mama repeated, uncertainly.

"Mr. Lawrence, the postmaster, said he couldn't get them all in your post-office box so since some were addressed to us in care of your box he just gave us ours when we came in for the Salvation Army mail."

"Yours?" Mama asked cautiously, afraid to explore the extremely touchy subject of whether Marian Miller smoked cigarettes.

"Yes. Both the Major and I received cartons of Lucky Strikes. In fact, the Major has received a carton a week for the last three weeks. I've got only two. Since neither of us is addicted to the nicotine habit Mr. Lawrence is taking all our cartons off our hands at a dollar each. He seems pleased and we're delighted. It's just like finding five dollars!"

Mama leaned against a display of Crisco to steady herself. "Who . . . *else* . . . got them?" she ventured.

"Teresa did. That was cute the way you put Miller down for her last name when you didn't know what it was! Teresa wants to keep hers and we can't say anything to her—but the Major and I are praying about it. Fats got a carton, bless his heart. He hasn't bought himself a package of cigarettes in years and years, and now he has ten! Steve got his but you made a mistake on Captain Bledsoe. . . ."

Mama didn't know what Mrs. Miller was talking about but she felt that she was somehow supposed to know so she said as little as possible. "Mistake?"

"Yes. The carton was addressed to *Jerry* Bledsoe. Jerry's only ten years old and I pray he never smokes a cigarette in his whole life. Captain's first name is Earl but it all worked out all right as we knew he was the one you meant to have them." She hesitated. "Corporal Wade got hers, too."

Mama almost knocked the Crisco pyramid over as she jerked herself erect and protested, "Marian! *I* wouldn't send a carton of cigarettes to dear Mary Wade! There must be some mistake."

"She's *flattered*," Mrs. Miller said reassuringly. "She's parceling the cigarettes out to the transients when they help with the chores. The dormitory is the cleanest it's ever been."

Mama seemed to be memorizing the label on the Crisco can so Mrs. Miller asked, "Do you like Crisco better than Spry?"

"I always know where I'm going with Crisco," Mama said lamely, reaching for a three-pound can from the display. "There's Lewis over by the check stand waiting for me. He's got friends from the East visiting him on the farm (she couldn't bring herself to say ranch) and I know he wants to get out there. I promised him a devil's food cake if he'd drive me into town to get groceries."

After Mrs. Miller had thanked her once more Mama finally got away.

"It's about time!" I said to Mama, impatiently. "What were you and Mrs. Miller gabbing about over there?"

"About Crisco—among other things," Mama said picking up the smallest sack of groceries while I carried the two large ones. "I told her I always know where I'm going with Crisco . . . which is more than I can say about *Lucky Strike cigarettes!*"

"Did you get some good things to eat?" I asked, changing

the subject. "Perry and Hal think you're the greatest cook in the world." Perry and Hal were college friends who lived in New York City. It was their second summertime visit to the ranch. My sister Pearl was visiting our married sister in St. Louis that summer so it was just Mama, Papa, my brother, Perry, Hal and me.

I prattled all the way to the car but as I started to turn the key in the ignition switch Mama touched her hand to it and said, "Wait a minute. Before you start this car I want to know who sent a carton of Lucky Strike cigarettes to little Jerry Bledsoe."

"*Jerry Bledsoe?* Why, that was three weeks ago! I took a wild chance on 'When Did You Leave Heaven' and 'There's a Small Hotel' for One and Two and they *won.* I *thought* I had a winner that week but I didn't get my cigarettes. Who got them?"

Mama was beginning to see the light.

"Jerry Bledsoe got them. Postmaster Lawrence gave them to his daddy because they had Jerry's name on them. It so happens that Jerry Bledsoe is ten years old. Couldn't you at least have ordered them for the Captain?"

"You don't *order* them, Mama. You *guess.* I sent in one for Captain Bledsoe that week but I put 'There's a Small Hotel' first and that was wrong. It was second." The enormity of Mr. Lawrence's action hit me. "A postmaster has no right to give our mail to other people! Somebody could *report* him for that. Those cigarettes were ours. They were supposed to be put into the Max Meyer Ranch Box. Box 27."

The light was dazzling now. Mama knew all.

"Something is rotten in the state of Denmark! And there I stood like a dummy while Marian Miller thanked me for sending her *cigarettes!*"

"I put her and the Major and a few others down for 'When Did you Leave Heaven?' as Number One and 'Take My Heart' for Number Two. It was a wild guess, Mama. I didn't expect them to win. Honest!"

"They won," Mama said. "They sure won." She looked at me. "How did you know Teresa's last name?"

"I didn't. I called her—"

"I know what you called her," Mama said, shaking her head resignedly. "You called her Miller. What sort of wild guess brought *that* out?"

"I took a chance on 'Goody Goody,'" I confessed, sheepishly. "Sure enough, it was Number Five that week. Can I start the car now?"

Mama nodded. "Stop by the post office first. I want to see if we have any mail."

"Not now, Mama. I'm in a hurry. I'll drive in later to get the mail."

"Now," Mama said decisively. "It may take two of us to carry the morning mail to the car."

"Aw, Mama. Sure you want to go to the post office *now*?"

"Absolutely," she said absolutely. "Maybe I'll win some cigarettes and teach myself to smoke."

"You just might, at that," I said, starting the car.

"Goody, goody," Mama said, looking holes through me.

In those days, dinner was at noon, supper at six. People referred to the midday meal as "heavy" and supper was always "light." A light meal forty years ago would probably be called a heavy dinner today. As for those admittedly heavy noontime feasts—well, people don't eat as much as they used to!

"Leave your father to me," Mama promised as she cooked

dinner. I had told her the whole truth about the contest and once she had recovered from the shock of our shakedown she agreed to stand by us. "You heard Postmaster Lawrence say he was going to have to talk to Papa today, so we've got to be prepared. Leave Max to me. I know how to handle him so's he won't get upset. It's after he's upset that nobody can do a thing with him."

Mama's secret weapon was called noodle soup. Papa adored noodle soup and you could count on Mama serving it at a time of emergency. There was a huge kettleful simmering away on one of the back burners.

My brother Manny, my friends Perry and Hal, and I were sitting on opposite sides of the long dining table waiting for Papa when Manny spied him walking up from Ernie Cooper's house. Manny ran into the kitchen and alerted Mama who timed her entrance with a large bowl of noodle soup to coincide with Papa's climb up the flight of steps to the screened-in dining porch.

"Start eating while it's hot, Max," she said, setting the soup in front of him. "In the words of William Shakespeare, 'I pray thou likest it!'" Then she said to me, matter-of-factly, "Come and help me serve the other soups, honey." I was delighted to leave the table as Papa sat down.

Papa was a soup slurper. He could eat as neatly as the next man when he put on his company manners away from home, but when he was enjoying his noon meal on his own open-air dining porch with only his wife and four assorted boys at the table with him he ate noisily—first blowing on the soup to cool it, then giving it a resounding slurp before swallowing it.

It is a rare experience, bordering on the occult, for a child to be able to disassociate himself from his own universe long

enough to appraise one parent through another parent's eyes.
It was given to me to do that very thing at that very moment. I saw my father as my mother saw him: handsome,
brown from the sun, too broad in the shoulders for the faded
blue short-sleeved sport shirt he was wearing, his thick, black,
curly head diving for those spoonfuls of noodle soup, loving
what he was eating and loving Mama for cooking it for him.
I could see in that instant out of time why she loved him so
much (and she *did*). In spite of his mulishness, his temper,
his tendency to explode, he was a kind of god to her. She
loved his eyes (misted at that moment with noodley happi-
ness), she loved his strength, his virility, his almost gruff
heartiness, his ability to enjoy life and food and—yes, herself.

"Get your daddy some more soup," Mama said to Manny.
Then, "Is it salty enough, Max?"

Papa nodded. His nod was enough for her. "Funny thing
happened this morning," he said between slurps. "I was in
the post office—"

My spoon suddenly turned, spilling soup all the way down
my shirt front.

"—minding my own business when Ted Lawrence walked
up and asked me how long we'd been taking in roomers."

"Roomers?" I asked. In an effort to sound casual my voice
cracked as though it was changing all over again.

Papa continued. "I said to Ted, 'What the hell . . .'" He
stopped himself, glanced at Perry and Hal, and modestly
changed the word. "I said, 'What the heck do you mean? You
know damned . . . darned . . . good and well I don't take in
roomers.'"

As he was talking, Papa's attention was drawn to a thin,
angular woman wearing a checked gingham dress and a sun-

bonnet. She was standing in front of Ernie Cooper's house. "So Ted goes on to say that he's been getting lots of packages for people who are supposed to live on my ranch, and then he said he had to discuss it with me privately and then he went to answer his telephone and that was the last I heard from him."

Papa left his seat at the head of the table, walked over to the screened wall and yelled at the woman, "Hey, Kate! How's Ernie now?"

Kate yelled back in a loud, nasal Oklahoma twang. "He's passed out. I know where he got the money. He's been hiding cigarettes."

"Can't make out what that woman's saying," Papa said. "Sounds like 'he's hiding cigarettes.' Doesn't make sense. Ernie doesn't smoke." He started to ask her what she meant but because he liked soup hot he muttered under his breath, "Oh, *hell!*" then yelled to Kate, "When he wakes up, tell Ernie I want to see him," and went back to his slurping.

Perry, Hal, my brother, Mama and I were sitting on needles. Papa was getting closer and closer to the facts of the cigarette swindle. So far, we had managed to load the car with prize-winning cartons before Papa went to Box 27 for his mail. More than once we had used a carton of cigarettes as an inducement to get Ernie Cooper to stop what he was doing and drive into town to get the mail for us. In the light of Kate's discovery, Ernie had evidently held out a few cartons to trade them for booze. Perry and Hal looked guilty because they had given many cartons to Ernie for saddling their horses and rolling the tennis courts when they wanted to play. Ernie had obviously converted Luckies to liquids (a pint to the carton?) and we had unwittingly contributed to Ernie's present state of unconsciousness by loading him up with what he had used to get loaded on.

"One of you boys can help me take the soup plates to the kitchen and bring out the rest of the food," Mama said. All four of us jumped up at once.

Papa became quieter as the meal progressed. The steady, warm breeze acted as a kind of soporific and the baked chicken, laced with garlic, the corn bread and the black-eyed peas lulled him into a state bordering on nirvana. He finished his cherry cobbler, rose slowly from the table, unbuckled his belt two notches and announced, "I'm going upstairs and stretch out for a few minutes. Don't let me sleep too long, Annie." Then, pausing at the kitchen door, he turned around, gave Mama a soulful look and said, "Annie, in the history of the world no man ever et a better dinner than I just et."

Mama, who had been reared in a grammatical household where nobody split an infinitive, looked momentarily flustered at Papa's colloquial compliment. Then she carefully leaned one arm onto the table, rested her chin in her cupped hand and looked into his eyes as she answered, "Thank you, darlin'. That was a sweet thing to say."

No sooner had Papa disappeared then my fifteen-year-old brother, Manny, leaned both arms on the table, rested his chin on both cupped hands and, mimicking Mama's drawl, said, "If y'all don't mind, I think I'll throw up!"

Postmaster Lawrence and the bald-headed man arrived while Papa was asleep. They didn't understand about driving all the way around the house to get to the side door. They parked in the front driveway by the flagpole, climbed awkwardly onto the circular cement fountain and balanced themselves on its rim until they could jump down from it onto the sidewalk leading to the front stone steps. My friends and I were on the porch swing and we stared at the visitors in that silent, incommunicative way youth has of playing dumb in front of strangers.

"Hello, Lewis," Mr. Lawrence said. "Tell your daddy I want to see him."

He didn't offer to introduce the bald-headed man so I didn't offer to introduce Perry and Hal.

Since Papa was still upstairs snoring away it was Mama who asked the men to come in, offered them refreshments (which they politely refused) and suggested that maybe she could help in some way.

The boys and I pretended to be talking and swinging but in reality we were listening to every word through one of the windows opening onto the porch.

"Mrs. Meyer," Postmaster Lawrence began, "this is Mr. William Simmons of New York City."

"I knew a Simmons family back home," Mama said guilelessly. "Do you have any relatives in Taro, Texas?"

"I'm afraid not," Mr. Simmons said stiffly. He was plainly ill at ease in his mohair suit, his dress shirt and necktie. Mama remembered one of Papa's pet expressions: Only an Easterner or a damned fool wears a suit coat in Oklahoma in August.

"Mr. Simmons is with the agency that handles the advertising for the American Tobacco Company."

"I'm sorry, but nobody in our family smokes," Mama said in the half-apologetic tone of voice one reserves for salesmen.

"I'm with the Hit Parade," Mr. Simmons said, taking out of his pocket several sheets of paper. "We've been sending prizes through the mail to a great many entries from your address. You might say I'm a kind of troubleshooter, Mrs. Meyer."

"Troubleshooter?"

"Yes. Quite a few people around the country are abusing my company's generosity. It looks like we're going to have to discontinue cartons as Hit Parade prizes and substitute flat fifties in their place."

When the swing sitters heard that bit of news we hooted. Flat fifties! Who'd go to the trouble of entering all those names for one fourth of a carton prize? Perry expressed our sentiments as he held his nose and said, "Phooey!"

Mr. Simmons continued talking in the same businesslike way. "I asked your postmaster to bring me here to verify some of these names."

"Names?" Mama asked blankly. "Maybe I'd better go wake up my husband."

This sent shivers up the eavesdroppers' spines. My brother nudged me and I yelled from the porch, "Need me for anything, Mama?"

Mama walked over to the open front door and spoke to us through the screen. "Go around the house to the back door, get the plate of table scraps I set on the kitchen counter and feed Junior. Maybe all four of you had better go." Without changing the motherly expression on her face Mama gave us a slow wink. We took the hint and left the porch but lingered near the side-door screen where we could hear what was said.

"Now," Mr. Simmons continued in his strained voice, "let's begin with this group of names: Max Meyer, Annie Meyer, Beatrice Meyer, Pearl Meyer, Lewis Meyer, Manny Meyer. I presume these are the family names at this address."

Mama started to explain that Pearl was visiting Bea in

St. Louis but then she'd have to go into Bea's married name, which was Mrs. Harold Miller, and since Bea had been entered in the Hit Parade as Beatrice Meyer it might get confusing, so Mama just answered Mr. Simmons by nodding affirmatively.

"Other winners at this same address have been Bea Miller (Mama congratulated herself on keeping her mouth shut), Harold Miller, Richard Miller, Ann Miller, Lena Miller, Hattie Miller, Joseph Miller, Tillie Miller, Terry Miller, Nanny Miller (Who in the world is *that?* Mama wondered) and Michael Miller. Do they live here, too?"

Mama knew exactly what we had done. We had used both Bea's married and single names plus the names of her husband, Harold, and their two children, Richard and Ann. The others were Harold's St. Louis brothers and sisters. Mama was encouraged to learn that the names (with the possible exception of Nanny) all belonged to real people.

Instead of answering Mr. Simmons' question about residence Mama asked cagily, "Do people have to *live* at an address to qualify for one of your prizes?"

Mr. Lawrence was impressed with Mama's question and repeated it. "Yes, Simmons. Do people have to live at an address to be eligible for a prize?"

Even though Mama had given him the wildly slipcovered yellow chair by the south window where hot wind poured in on him, Mr. Simmons was sweating pitifully. The neckband of his shirt collar was wet through and there were large perspiration circles under each arm of his black suit coat. Mama actually thought of suggesting to him that he remove his coat and tie but she decided that this was no time to be giving assistance to the enemy.

Mr. Simmons pondered his answer. "No, a winner wouldn't

have to *live* at an address but at least he should have some sort of *identification* with the address."

Mama was relieved to hear him say that. She could certainly *identify* the Millers! "The Millers are in the family. They drive over from Missouri all the time to visit us. Plenty of room here, as you can see. Nothing to do at night but listen to the radio."

Mr. Simmons conceded nothing. "Then who are these *other* Millers who have entered every week's contest: Major Miller, Marian Miller, Fats Miller, Steve Miller, Teresa Miller . . ."

Mr. Lawrence interrupted him. "I can identify them. They are all friends of the Meyers and used the Meyer post-office box because the Salvation Army is General Delivery. I delivered their prizes myself."

"Salvation Army?" Mr. Simmons asked. "The whole Salvation *Army*?"

"No. Just the names you read plus Mary Wade and the Bledsoes. . . ."

"Bledsoe!" Mr. Simmons remembered the name and searched through the list until he found it. "Here it is. Jerry Bledsoe." He sounded unsure of himself as he checked the name but continued doggedly: "Who are all these people at this same address? Ernie Cooper, Kate Cooper, Fanny Cooper, Patricia Cooper, Tom Cooper, Cordelia Cooper, Viola Cooper and Ophelia Cooper?"

"They all live right here on the place and they all have a right to enter your old contest," Mama said forcefully, putting her hands in her lap so neither of the visitors could see her crossed fingers. She had thrown in the word "old" because she was now having trouble with identification. Fanny, Patricia and Tom were some of the children of Papa's tenant farmers on WPA Row. As for Cordelia, Viola and

121

Ophelia, if Mama got out of this alive she might have something of interest to report at the next meeting of her Shakespeare Club.

The name game continued. Perry and Hal were next and their parents and brothers and sisters were easy to figure out. Every one who had ever worked in Papa's store, plus Beulah, Beulah's Sister and their friends had been entered. Mama lumped them all together under the heading, "Employees of the ranch."

Mr. Simmons was beginning to weaken but he tried not to show it. "The name Levy," he began, "keeps cropping up at this address. There are dozens of Levys. Sam Levy has been a consistent winner and Julius Levy and Izzy Levy and . . ." He skipped down the long list of Levys. "Who is Mabel Levy?"

If Ethel Barrymore had played Scarlett O'Hara she would have sounded the way Mama did as she replied, "Mabel Levy is *mah sistuh!*"

Somehow that one retort seemed to take care of all the contestants named Levy from Box 27. Mr. Simmons knew when to quit. "There's just one more question mark," he began. "And that's—"

As he ran his index finger down the sheet to find the name he was seeking, Junior, who had finished his meal, dashed into the living room with the four of us chasing him. He went straight to Mr. Simmons and placed his paws on the black mohair knees.

"Junior! Down!" Mama commanded. "Boys!" she called. "Get that dog out of here right now!"

"Sorry, Mama," my brother apologized. "Come on, Junior." When the dog refused to budge from his perch on Mr.

Simmons' kneecaps, my brother put more force into his order and shouted, *"Junior!"*

"Here it is." Mr. Simmons had found the name. "Junior Meyer. Who's that?"

Mama was trapped and she knew it. Her only hope was to change the subject and this she did by seizing the initiative and saying, almost curtly, "Mr. Simmons, if your company is insinuating that we have used the mails to defraud then I'd better wake up my husband. He'll want to call his lawyer." She looked at me. "Sonny, go wake your father."

Mr. Simmons was most earnestly protesting and apologizing to Mama as I ran out of the room and bumped into Ernie Cooper on my way to the staircase. I skidded to a stop on the bottom step, turned to Ernie and said, "Don't go in there."

"And why not?" Ernie was belligerent.

I couldn't say, "Because you're skunk drunk," so I said, "Because you shouldn't, that's why not."

"Max told me to come see him and I've come to see him," Ernie asserted as he wove his way past me toward the living room.

Mama didn't know whether to laugh or cry when Ernie appeared. His hair went impartially in every direction. His eyes were totally bloodshot. He was wearing a soiled sport shirt that had somehow lost all of its buttons except the top one and had gaped open wide enough to reveal most of his bare, skinny stomach, including his navel. His pants were out of Robinson Crusoe, by Huck Finn. He was barefoot and somewhere along the line he had stubbed his big toe.

Mama had a wild notion to introduce Ernie by saying, "Mr. Overdressed Simmons meet Mr. Underdressed Cooper," but she settled for propriety. "Ernie, you know Ted Lawrence from the post office and this is Mr. Simmons from Lucky Strikes. This is Ernie Cooper."

Both Mr. Simmons and Mr. Lawrence stood like gentlemen. Ernie belched.

Mr. Simmons, who was cracking under the pressure, turned to Postmaster Lawrence and said, "This guy's as drunk as he can be." Then he walked over to Ernie, took a package of Luckies from his inside coat pocket and asked, "Want a cigarette?"

Ernie reeled over to Mr. Simmons, stuck his face to within a millimeter of Simmons' face and said indignantly, "I don't smoke. Wanna make something of it?"

The fumes from Ernie, coupled with the heat in the room, caused Mr. Simmons to grow green. For a moment it seemed he was going to be sick on the spot. He backed off but as he did so Ernie stalked him, breathing fire. "I said I don't smoke, jerk. Wanna fight or somethin'?"

"Ernie!" Mama said. "You don't know what you're saying. Tell Mr. Simmons you're sorry." She turned to Ted Lawrence. "Make Ernie apologize."

It was too much for Mr. Lawrence. He began to laugh and he couldn't stop. Mama saw him laughing and got tickled herself. She hated to laugh at people to their faces but it was one way to cope with the strain.

Ernie didn't see anything funny in it. "I ain't sorry, Mrs. Meyer. How can I 'pologize if I ain't one bit sorry?"

Mr. Simmons kept retreating as Ernie marched toward him. "If I insulted you, then I apologize. I'll send you a carton of Lucky Strikes—free."

"Lucky Strikes? Like hell you'll send me Lucky Strikes. Them's what got me in all the trouble." He pointed a finger in Mr. Simmons' face. "*You* got me in all this trouble."

Mr. Simmons backed too quickly onto the arm of the over-stuffed chair, lost his balance and fell down. Papa walked into the room, saw a bald-headed stranger sprawled on the floor, saw Mama giggling and Ted Lawrence laughing his head off. As for Ernie Cooper, nothing Ernie did surprised Papa.

"Ernie!" Papa barked. Ernie stopped his advance, looked meekly at Papa, opened his mouth to protest but closed it again, then started to cry. It was a crazy sort of crying. More blubber than tears.

Papa walked over to Ernie and put his arm around his shoulder. This gesture pulled up the open shirt until Ernie appeared half naked. As Papa led Ernie out through the front door he yelled over his shoulder, "For God's sake, Annie, tell that man on the floor to take off his coat and tie—and offer him a drink of whiskey. He looks sick."

As it turned out, Papa's strategy was the right one. Only it wasn't liquor Mr. Simmons needed. It was food. He hadn't eaten a bite all day. The minute he was out of his coat and necktie and was sitting on the dining porch in front of a bowl of Mama's noodle soup he turned out to be a nice guy. He ate like a starved man and even though he gave the soup his undivided attention he didn't slurp once. "Best soup I ever ate," he kept saying. "What's your secret, Mrs. Meyer?"

"Skim off the top so it'll be rich but not greasy," Mama said. "Why didn't you tell me you were hungry? Let me get you some more."

While Mama was in the kitchen, Ted Lawrence asked Mr. Simmons if he was satisfied with his findings.

"Certainly," Mr. Simmons answered. "These are wonderful people. All of them." He frowned. "All of them except that half-naked, half-baked, half-assed beachcomber they call

Ernie." Then he added confidentially, "Tell me just one thing, Ted. Is Junior Meyer who I *think* Junior Meyer is?"

Ted Lawrence nodded his head, put his finger to his lips . . . and barked.

Bill Simmons smiled as he tore the lists of names in two and handed Ted Lawrence the pieces to throw away. "Rich but not greasy," he said as Mama placed more noodle soup before him. "What a pity you don't smoke, Mrs. Meyer. I'd love to send you a carton of Luckies."

The Hit Parade was never the same after that. I did enter one more time, even though the prize was only a flat fifty. I used my own name, too, and tried my darndest. I guessed "I'm an Old Cowhand" as Number One, followed by "There's a Small Hotel," "For Sentimental Reasons," "Until the Real Thing Comes Along" and "Goody Goody" in that order. As it turned out, I didn't win a thing. "I've Got a Feelin' You're Foolin'" knocked "Goody Goody" out of the top five that week. Mama said it served me right.

5. Send Me a Postcard When You Reach the Top

Memories of our parents after we are grown are like pictures in an album. Most of us carry these albums with us wherever we go. Since time loses its importance once we learn to look backward, our memories are a hodgepodge of stills and tableaux without sequence. We steal isolated rememberings out of our enormous past as children steal raisins from a rice pudding. Oh, and the loveliest part about remembering is that the oldest memory is as fresh as the most recent. We also reserve the right to color our mental pictures as they ought to be instead of as they were. Mama's hair is always black, Mama's face has a soft smile, her hands are always busy, her voice insistent with the Texas accent she never gave up.

I went to a psychic once in Ireland. She asked me if I knew that my parents were always with me. Not just with me figuratively, she meant it literally. I think I surprised her by saying, "Yes, I knew it." There is nothing strange or mystical about their closeness. I often hear my father's laugh, I hear him snore, I hear him demonstrate his noisy appreciation for good food. As the psychic reader described Mama's brown eyes, her long hair combed tightly back from her forehead into the hairpinned bun, her refusal to wear any jewelry save her gold wedding band and the diamond earrings, her small, vital figure—I saw Mama as clearly as though she was in the room with us. She was.

Pictures alone are not enough. Family memories must be tasted, smelled, felt and heard as well as seen. That is why our minds are equipped with tape machines which we punch on or off at will to bring back the sights and sounds and feelings recorded years ago.

Mama was a fountainhead of homilies, adages and precepts, and I know that she would like to be remembered for the things she told us and taught us as we grew up. Where Papa stuck pretty much to one motto: Be sure you're right, then go ahead! (he credited Davy Crockett with it and it sounds like Davy, doesn't it?), Mama had a pet saying for every situation. The ones I remember best have sustained me, kept me afloat, saved my neck, stood me well. I find myself constantly hitting that on button and playing them back. Writing them down on paper isn't fair to Mama because only part of the remembering is in the words themselves. Her inflections as she said them gave them force and meaning. But here are a few of her prize quotations from my own mental-picture scrapbook. Try them on for size.

It's not the fool who asks—it's the fool who gives.

The conviction in Mama's voice as she gave us that advice left no doubt as to its efficacy. How many times did we hear her repeat it? At least a thousand and one. Mama intended the words to mean much more than just How to Get What You Want. They were a way of life. "*Ask*," she'd say. "Don't be afraid to *ask*. . . . Remember: It's not the fool who *asks*. . . ." And then she'd pause for one of us to finish the sentence for her. It might be a childish chant or a grownup's automatic response but someone always supplied the missing words: "It's the fool who gives."

I've lived my whole life by that credo, my own children are living theirs by it, and I do not doubt that their children will hear it from the cradle to college and beyond. I recommend it to you and yours. Yea, I guarantee it!

Before you can use this favorite aphorism of Mama's there are definite ground rules to comply with. First of all (and Mama insisted on this) you must not go around asking promiscuously for anything that pops into your mind. You have to *want* what you ask for, really and truly want it. And the thing you ask for must be *worthy*. Even if you want it desperately you have no right to ask for something that isn't, as Mama put it, "right." "*But*," she'd repeat for emphasis, "if you want something in the worst way and there is nothing objectionable to it . . . then *ask*. The worst that can happen will be a refusal and you won't be any worse off than you were before you asked."

Mama's motto turned out to be a first-rate course in other people's behavior. Whenever someone made an audacious request or had the nerve to ask for something outrageous Mama never got mad about it. She just shrugged, laughed, shook her head and then reminded us that "It's not the fool who *asks*. . . ."

When it came to applying her principle, Mama was her own best advocate. During the Depression, when the mortgage on the Salvation Army Hut was overdue and Major Miller was resigned to a foreclosure, Mama got busy asking. Beginning with the president of the American National Bank and ending with the editor of the Sapulpa *Herald* she succeeded in raising enough money to save the Hut, to reroof it and to have a victory banquet. Papa—who had agreed to contribute five hundred dollars before he knew what hit him —complained about Mama's "steam-roller tactics." "It's not the fool who asks, dear," she said, folding his check and adding it to the other donations, "it's the fool who gives." And then she added hastily, "But in this instance a gift is a wise and worthy blessing." By choosing three of Papa's favorite words: "wise," "worthy" and "blessing" Mama had reassured him that he had done the right thing.

I swear to you that Mama's motto works on both ends: whether you be the one who asks—or the one who has to refuse. Refusing is easier than asking, and asking needs encouragement. Without Mama's motto I might never have . . . well, take my wife, for example. Who would ever believe that a smart girl like that would accept a proposal of marriage from a man she'd known less than a week? (An *older* man.) (Set in his ways, of course.) (Stubborn, too!) But I qualified for Mama's advice by (1) really and truly wanting what I asked for and (2) asking for something worthy. So I *asked* and the answer was Yes!

I think I'll tattoo those words upon my chest—or wear them as a lighted sign upon my head: IT'S NOT THE FOOL WHO ASKS—IT'S THE FOOL WHO GIVES.

A child will ask until he gets a No.

When I was young, parents brought up children without the help of child psychology books. Dr. Spock had not emerged to focus his spotlight upon the child as the hub of the family, the earth, the universe. Haim Ginott was a full generation away with his advice on "How to live with children in mutual respect and dignity."

I'm positive that Mama would have been violently un-Spockian and definitely non-Ginotty. She would have read their books and come up with a juicy Shakespearean quote like "Good God! Why should they mock poor fellows thus?"

Mama didn't believe that the child was the center of anything. She believed that the father and the mother were the hub, center and axle that kept the family wheel revolving and the child was a spoke in that wheel. As for "mutual respect and dignity" Mama believed it started at the top, not at the bottom. Parents were entitled to respect and dignity from their children. Children had to earn respect and dignity by behaving like decent people. Mama looked at it this way: "Don't try to reason with a three-year-old lying on the floor having a temper tantrum. Spank his behind."

What was the climate in the home B.S. (Before Spock) or B.G. (Before Ginott)? Was there less love then between parents and children? I say there was more. Left to their own devices, without the Spockian middleman to lean on, mothers and fathers used the trial and error system and had their successes and failures with children firsthand. It worked. And it worked because parents "did it themselves" instead of running to the experts.

Once, when Mama was in charge of the program at the Shakespeare Club, she chose as her subject, "Shakespeare and Children." She began with some appropriate quotations about young people—"Is this the generation of love? hot blood? hot thoughts and hot deeds?" *Troilus and Cressida,* and "How sharper than a serpent's tooth it is to have a thankless child," *King Lear*—but she closed her talk with a sourceless quotation which said what she herself believed:

A child will ask until he gets a No. Her entire approach to bringing up children was in those few words: *A child will ask until he gets a No.* Mama believed that a child not only needs discipline, he craves it. She felt that a well-timed No was as effective as a beating with a belt. In those days the father of the family usually handled the whippings but the Nos could be dished out by both parents.

Even before a best-selling psychologist had coined the word "permissiveness" Mama had the answer to it. We were "allowed" but we weren't "permitted." There was a difference. When Mama said, "No," it was No. Not maybe, not beg-harder-dear, not go-ahead-and-do-it-anyway. She said No and she meant No.

"Fail to discipline a child and you'll have a monster on your hands," Mama said. And then she added with conviction, "Show me a little hellion and when he grows up I'll show you a big hellion!"

When we didn't get our way, my sisters cried and my brother and I swore (he said darn, but I was older so I said damn). Even so, we didn't become rebellious. There was a comfort in knowing for sure what the answer was and what we were supposed to do.

We were threatened a lot and most of the threats came under the heading of scare propaganda because they never materialized. When Bea brought her children with her to the ranch for a summertime visit she complained to Mama about them. "Ann won't practice her piano," she said. "And just look at Richard. He's been tormenting Junior all day by pulling his tail. What a brat!"

Mama resented criticism of her grandchildren, even by their own mother. "Your children aren't brats," Mama said. "They are better than most. The trouble with you, Bea, is that you don't put your foot down firmly enough with them. You try to reason with them and they don't want to reason. Try threatening them. A child likes to be threatened by someone who loves him."

"You can't mean that, Mama."

"I can and I do. I threatened you. My mother threatened me. Speaking for myself, I liked it. A threat is just another form of discipline—and a child wants to be disciplined. He knows then where he . . . where he *fits*."

It was still too early for the words "feeling secure" and that was a pity because Mama would have loved to use that phrase. After all, what she was saying was simply that discipline makes a child feel secure!

"I think you overdisciplined us," Bea protested. "Threatening us with punishment took away our individuality."

"You may be a wife and mother," Mama said, "but what you need is a spanking for talking such nonsense."

"But, Mama. Children shouldn't be ordered around like slaves. Children are people. You just don't go around threatening people with dire things if they misbehave."

"Oh, *don't* you?" As she said the words Mama walked to the cabinet and took out a Holy Bible she had brought with her from Taro years ago. "I keep this Bible in the cabinet. Your father doesn't exactly approve of it because it contains both Old and New Testaments. He has nothing against the New Testament. He just isn't sure it's supposed to be in a Jewish home."

Mama turned to Chapter 30 of Deuteronomy and handed the Bible to Bea. "Read out loud."

"Mama!"

"Read it."

Bea read, "'I command thee this day to love the Lord thy

God, to walk in his ways, and to keep his commandments and his statutes and his judgments, that thou mayest live and multiply; and the Lord thy God shall bless thee in the land whither thou goest to possess it. But if thine heart turn away, so that thou wilt not hear, but shalt be drawn away, and worship other gods, and serve them; I denounce unto you this day, that ye shall surely perish—'"

"That's enough," Mama said. "God wasn't above using threats to whip people into line. Why should a parent be afraid to follow his example?"

Mama put the Bible away but she shook her head as she did so. It was her way of showing that she wasn't sure she had won her point.

It was not until later that day, when Mama heard Bea scream at Richard, "All right, mister! One more pull on Junior's tail and I'm giving you the spanking of a lifetime!" that Mama sighed with relief and mumbled gratefully, "I know that my Redeemer liveth."

Even though Papa was the Keeper of the Strap, Mama was the Chief Disciplinarian. I lost the use of my bicycle for two weeks when Mama learned that I had been smoking cubebs with my pal, Billy Longmire. My mistake was in chewing orange peel to cover up the smoke smell. The traces of orange in my teeth and on my mouth made Mama suspicious. I considered the punishment cruel and excessive but it cured me of cubebs.

Other punishments ranged from early bedtime to no Saturday afternoon movie at the St. Denis Theatre. I pretended to be as upset as my sisters were over the loss of the St. Denis privilege but I secretly considered it a godsend. I liked movies but I despised the St. Denis. I wanted to go to the Empress across the street. The Empress played cowboy pictures, but my sisters didn't like Westerns so the four of us children went to the St. Denis every Saturday afternoon.

A terrible woman named Mrs. Lovely owned the St. Denis Theatre. Mrs. Lovely used her Saturday matinee customers as a captive audience for her own thwarted theatrics. Before she'd let the projectionist begin the show, Mrs. Lovely paced wildly up and down the center aisle reciting "Little Orphant Annie." She emoted it from 'way down deep . . . shaking her finger menacingly as she hit that refrain about "the gobble uns will git you ef you don't watch out." Sometimes Mrs. Lovely had to hold onto the row of seats to steady herself and her voice was so slurred we couldn't understand half of what she said. It wasn't until years later, when I myself began to experience some of the same difficulties that beset Mrs. Lovely, that I realized the old girl was so staggering drunk she thought she saw real gobble uns and was probably running for her life.

One of the few times Mama failed to punish me sufficiently was when she walked onto the front porch one morning and found Billy and me playing doctor with Helen Hansen as the patient. Helen lived across the street from us. While Helen was our age, she was living proof that girls develop faster than boys. The doctor game was her idea and she made it plain that she would play only if she could be the patient.

When I looked up from the operating table and saw Mama I said, "Hello, Mama. Billy and I are operating on Helen."

All Mama could think to say before running back into the house was, "Be good boys and don't hurt Helen."

It wasn't two minutes later that Mrs. Hansen, Helen's mother, came charging onto the porch from across the street, pulled Helen up from her reclining position on the front porch swing and heatedly accused Billy and me of being "naughty little devils."

Mama chose the day I graduated from law school to confess that she had gone to the telephone and called Mrs. Hansen because she herself didn't know what to say or do. "You were innocent children," she told me, "and it didn't seem right to punish children for being naturally curious about other children's bodies. Besides—" She sounded wistful as she looked at my diploma. "I thought you might want to be a doctor when you grew up."

Thanks to Mama, I never had to "find out who I was"— which is more than you can say for the boys and girls of the Spock-reared generation who are looking everywhere for proof of identity. I knew darned good and well who I was. More important, I knew who I wasn't.

I've followed Mama's rules of discipline with my own children and I am glad to report that they know who they are, too. I believe we have as much "mutual respect and dignity" for each other as the most Ginott-drilled parents and children. Most of the time it wasn't necessary for either of my daughters to have to ask until she got a No. When a No was called for, she got it without asking.

The other day I asked my college daughter if she felt we were too severe with our children. I loved her answer. "The best way to know yourself is for someone you love to No you!"

Children don't remember what you did for *them. They only remember what you did* with *them.*

Mama had a passionate conviction that it was a parent's business to know where her children were and what they were doing. My sisters, my brother and I knew better than to make individual plans without first clearing with Mama and Papa.

Mama especially liked for all of us to be together at mealtime. When we hinted at invitations to eat at other people's houses Mama always said, "Invite your friends to eat with us." Mealtime was more of an event then. Everyone was at the table when the soup was served, and nobody left the table until the last bite of dessert was eaten and we were dismissed. Today, when mealtime is a refueling stop between appointments, rehearsals, telephone conversations or dates it's hard to believe there was a time when the whole family sat down together and stayed put until the meal was officially over.

When a circus or carnival came to town all of us went together. Papa liked events like that but he suffered when he had to attend a concert or dramatic production. He mumbled about the seats being too narrow for him and the auditorium being too hot. But he never failed to go with Mama and the four children whenever a Lyceum or Chautauqua attraction came to town, be it a singer, speaker or soloist.

While Mama believed that children should be seen and not heard, each child got his share of attention. Since Mama's opera house experiences as a child had impressed upon her the virtue of being able to perform for others she insisted that we parade our talents whenever we had company. "It develops personalities," she said. My sister Pearl recited a monologue entitled "Conversation with a Fly," which ended with a resounding and sadistic slap and the words, "Good-bye, Fly!" Bea blizzarded us with "Snowflake Mazurka" on the piano. I submitted our guests to a runaway rendition of "A

Message to Garcia" and my brother, dressed in full cowboy regalia, did his thing by twirling a rope. If the grownups minded it all, they were too polite to show it, and it did develop our personalities—almost beyond recognition.

They say that the family who prays together, stays together. We not only prayed together in Papa's synagogue/temple/church, we ate together, played together and—if you don't take it too literally—we even slept together!

The huge sleeping porch of the house on Oak Street was a communal bedroom with each member of the family having his own bed and his own featherbed. People don't build houses with sleeping porches any more. It's much more civilized to have individual cubicle rooms where each child can be alone and lonely.

On that wonderful sleeping porch we children giggled and talked until we finally fell asleep. It was reassuring to have one of the parents come out to give us a pat and this wasn't hard to arrange.

"Maaaaaa-maaaaa!" Bea would yell in the direction of the back sitting room. "Make them shut up so I can go to sleeeeeep."

"Nobody's bothering her!" Manny would scream.

"Yes, they are!"

Finally Papa would storm out onto the porch. "What's going on here?"

"Nothing, Papa. Kiss me good night."

"Me, too."

"Me, too."

"Me, three."

Sleeping porch? Ask any present-day architect and he'll hoot at the words. "Do you want to spoil the *lines* of a house with a crazy community bedroom jutting out at one end? And what about a family's *privacy?*"

Face it. The sleeping porch is as extinct as the dodo bird. Architecturally, it is gone forever—and when this generation is gone there won't be anyone left who misses it. I, for one, miss it something fierce.

By current standards our family then was "close knit." Close-knit families today are out of the ordinary, almost freakish—but most families were close knit then. They moved, acted and thought as a unit. Maybe that's why so many people my age can't forget what home was all about. *Children don't remember what you did* for *them. They only remember what you did* with *them.*

Teach a man to swim and he'll drown you.

The first time I heard Mama speak those words I was indignant. "Mama! You can't really believe that. Why, you're always doing nice things for people . . . and you want us to do nice things for others, don't you?"

"It has nothing whatever to do with *helping* others," Mama explained. "It has to do with expecting favors because you helped them. Never expect someone you do something for to return a favor out of gratitude. If you know that you'll never be disappointed."

Once I began a sentence with "After all I did for him. . . ." Mama stopped me and then said quietly, "My father had an expression that I've found to be true: Teach a man to swim and he'll drown you. There's something about human nature that doesn't like to be obligated to somebody else, even though that other person has done you a big favor. Help others. But help them only out of kindness. If you expect something by way of gratitude you're going to be hurt."

I've never heard that expression from anyone else, but my children hear it occasionally from me. On the surface it does sound cruel and cynical. Mama didn't mean it that way. She was a realist, as her father must have been before her. *People don't like to be beholden.*

Mrs. Major Miller said to me once, "Your mother does a powerful amount of good . . . and she doesn't let anybody know about it."

Perhaps I should have repeated Mama's quotation to Mrs. Miller—because the Salvation Army works in pretty much the same, quiet, realistic way. Maybe that's what people mean when they talk about "Christian charity." Help others. But don't be surprised when those you help have short memories. That's the way the ball bounces.

"Send me a postcard when you reach the top."

If success is measured by results, then this was Mama's most successful thrust. It never failed to make its point.

Whenever Mama saw one of her children picking his nose she said pleasantly, "Send me a postcard when you reach the top."

The nosepicker sometimes grinned—sometimes he acted embarrassed—but he always stopped.

Who among us has not picked his nose? It is a source of comfort to many. But most nosepickers wait until they are offstage before indulging their whim.

The other day I stopped for a red light, glanced at the car in the next lane and noticed that the teen-aged boy in the driver's seat was absent-mindedly picking his nose.

I shouldn't have done it but I did.

I suddenly remembered Mama, all her preposterous say-
ings and this one in particular. I rolled down my window
and said in my pleasantest voice, "Send me a postcard when
you reach the top."

The boy got so flustered he stepped on the gas, ran the
red light and was gone for good.

But wherever he may be—now and forever—when he
picks his nose he'll remember those silly words. And who
can tell? Some day he may say pleasantly to one of his
own: "Send me a postcard when you reach the top."

6. Sma Faw

In lawyer language: Papa liked realty, Mama liked personalty.
In words of one syllable, Papa liked land, Mama liked *things*.
He wanted to walk on what he owned—kick the dirt, breathe
the air, see the sky and know that all of it—land, air, sky—
belonged to him as a matter of record in the Creek County,
Oklahoma Courthouse. The more land he owned, the bigger
he felt. When Uncle Ed accused him of being greedy, Papa
answered in that maddening way of his, "I'm not greedy, Ed.
All I want is just the little piece that joins what I've already
got."

Mama preferred possessions that she could see, fondle,
enjoy and then, if she wished, put away until next time.
Where Papa got his kicks from shaded squares on a map
with his name on them, Mama loved beautiful glass, fine
linens, delicate lace, gold filigree work and all manner of
things one could hold in the hand and savor their being
there.

Once a year Mama went to the bank in Tulsa to pay the

yearly rental on her safety deposit box. She could have sent
the payment by mail but she liked to go in person. It gave
her an excuse to look over her jewelry and to commune
with the past. She usually took my sisters with her. When
the boys protested their being left behind Mama reminded
us that jewelry was for men to buy and for women to
enjoy.

As soon as they returned home, my sisters rubbed salt in
our wounds by recounting everything that happened (and
some things that didn't). They told how the three of them
were shown into a dark mahogany paneled room, and how
they sat on straight chairs with green leather seats around a
polished wood table as Mama displayed her treasures and
let her daughters try on bracelets, rings and necklaces.

I had just opened my own law office when Mama finally
invited me to accompany her to the safe deposit box. "It's
time I had a will," she said, "and you can write it for me.
You can write down the description of each piece of jewelry
and I'll tell you who I want to have it."

"Mama—"

She knew how I felt about things like that. True, I was
a lawyer. But I was also my father's son and I swam in his
reservoir of superstitions.

"Don't be silly. It's just a will. I'll probably change it
twenty times in years to come. Call it a rough draft."

So I took along my tablet of yellow, legal-sized foolscap,
Mama showed her key, and the safe-deposit man led the
way first to the box and then to the private room. From my
sisters' accounts I had imagined a larger place. It was more
of a roomlet than a room, a paneled cubicle barely large
enough to accommodate the table that dominated it. The

girls were right about the chairs. They had good green leather seats.

Mama slowly lifted the lid of the black metal box and began to examine the pieces one by one. As she did so, I wrote down a description of each and the person Mama wanted to leave it to.

She began with a cameo brooch that had once been terracotta colored but now had a fragile, faded, yellowish look. "This belonged to my mother, your Grandma Lena. Her mother gave it to her before I was born. I never knew my grandmother."

"Put it on, Mama."

"Not here. Not in this silly little room. Still—"

She studied the cameo intently, as though she were seeing it as she remembered it, not as it was. "Why not?" she said and her fingers trembled slightly as she picked the proper spot at the base of the V of her neckline. She guided the fine point of the gold spear through the silk of her dress, locking the brooch fast with the catch which turned as easily for her now as it had for her mother's mother.

"It's beautiful," I said. "You ought to wear it, not leave it in this box."

Mama shook her head. "It's nice to own things, but it wouldn't look right to wear them in Sapulpa. I'd be scared someone would steal them. Besides, nobody likes a showy person."

"A thing of beauty is a joy forever," I said. "And that cameo becomes you."

Mama, conscious of the pink flush that tinged her neck, reached quickly into the box for another piece of jewelry. "Your father gave me this gold bracelet on our fifth wedding anniversary. He bought it in New York City when he went on a market trip for the store." She paused to set the memory. "That was the time he bought all those collarless shirts." She had the bracelet on her wrist now. "See how each of the gold links has a diamond in it? I've never seen a prettier bracelet."

One by one, I wrote down the descriptions as Mama supplied the human interest story behind each of them. There was a jeweled comb and some gold pieces her father had given her (*"Hide them, Annie. Forget them. I hope you never need them, but if you do, gold is better than money"*) and some postal savings certificates and a nickel in an envelope with the inscription, "Found by Annie Levy in a popcorn ball at a birthday party in Taro, Texas, Year, 1892," but mostly there were pieces of jewelry.

"This ring—isn't the diamond big?—always bothered me," she said. "I never felt it was mine to keep."

"Tell me about it."

"It was an engagement ring from a rich man in Dallas named Isadore Cohen."

I tried not to look surprised, I really did, but I didn't succeed because Mama laughed at the expression on my face.

"Not a very exciting name, is it? To tell you the truth, Isadore Cohen wasn't a very exciting man. He was *nice* but he wasn't exciting. Isadore was fifteen years older than I was. He was very thin and had a hacking cough. Every time I went into the kitchen Emma warned me not to kiss him. Said he had 'walking TB' and I'd catch it."

Mama paused and I got the feeling she wished she hadn't started the story. She knew I wouldn't let her stop now.

"The consensus of Levys was that my marrying Isadore was

a good thing, so it was all set. As soon as I graduated from Kidd Key College we were to be married."

She smiled. "And then your grandfather made the mistake of taking all of us to Hot Springs and I met Max who was my age. He was good-looking, healthy, and—well, *very* exciting. My father didn't speak to me for a whole week when I sent the ring back to Isadore with a letter saying I had decided not to marry him. It wasn't easy."

Mama looked at the ring. "You can imagine my surprise when I opened the front door. . . . It was a Sunday afternoon . . . and there was Isadore. He said he was sorry I'd changed my mind but he wanted me to have the ring anyway. He said he would be hurt if I didn't take it. I went into the next room and asked my father what I should do. Since he secretly hoped I'd get over Max and marry Isadore after all, he advised me to keep it."

I could tell she wanted to change the subject but I couldn't resist asking her what happened to Mr. Cohen.

"He died during the flu epidemic of 1918. I guess Emma was right."

She quickly replaced Isadore's diamond ring in the chamois bag it slept in and changed the subject. "Now *this* pin came from Linz's in Dallas. My mother willed it to me. And *this* one . . ."

There were a half-dozen rings, at least three brooches, a string of pearls and still another gold bracelet. Finally, there were only two items left. One was in a small cardboard box, the other was a bulge in an envelope.

Mama opened the box and took out a heart-shaped pin. I had heard my sisters describe most of the pieces I'd seen that day but I somehow had the feeling Mama had never shown them this one.

"Would it be selfish if I didn't leave this pin to anyone?" Mama asked hesitantly. "I'd like . . . I thought I'd just wear this one if . . . when . . ."

I knew what she meant and I nodded my head to tell her so.

"It's the least valuable of them all," she said apologetically. "Your father had very little money when he bought it." She cupped the pin in the palm of her hand. "I like it because it represents the first time in his whole life your father ever said he was sorry.

"We were in New Orleans on our honeymoon and Max got mad the way he does sometimes. I'd never seen him in a temper fit and I wasn't prepared for it. The whole thing started when one of the artists in Jackson Park kept bothering us to let him paint our pictures. I guess I must have encouraged him because your father not only got mad at the artist, he got mad at me, too. He started turning over park benches and making a spectacle of himself and when we got back to the hotel he started breaking things . . . the way he does . . . and . . ."

Mama shook her head. "I didn't understand him then. Now I do. It wasn't the pictures at all. He was suddenly worried about being married and making a living for me and having to live with the Levys who didn't like him and—well, once he got started he just couldn't stop. I left him and came home to Taro. It was a mean thing to do and I'm ashamed I did it. He followed me the next day and he brought me this." She looked at the pin. "He sat on the swing and held my hand and said he was sorry and *cried*. I told him Aunt Mamie and Cousin Izzy were watching us and he said let them watch and he kissed me and we made up and . . . well, that's it."

At last I knew what Aunt Becky had meant that time in Taro when she said to Mama, "You left him once." Aunt Becky just didn't understand Papa. Mama—all of us—had learned to adjust to his temper. When he started screaming and breaking things the only thing to do was get out of the way until he was over it. You couldn't be sure what he was mad at because he always picked a side issue like the Jackson Park artist to serve as his fuse.

I pointed my pencil first to the bulky envelope, then to my own pad of paper to show I was ready to list the last piece.

Mama opened the envelope and took out of it a multi-page letter, shuffling the pages quickly as she reread it. I could tell it was from Papa because there couldn't be another handwriting like his anywhere in the world. Broad, exaggerated strokes that were a cross between Hebrew letters and Egyptian hieroglyphics. Then she took from its nest of crumpled tissue paper a lavaliere on a platinum chain. The diamond in the center of the setting was at least five carats.

"Wow!" I said. "You saved the best for the last."

"Not the best," she said matter-of-factly. "The biggest and the most expensive—but not the best."

She let the necklace crumple into its paper, then put both it and the letter back into the envelope. After she told me what to write down she said, "Some day you'll read the letter that came with the lavaliere and you'll know why I like it least of all." She hesitated. "I guess every marriage has to have a low point. The lavaliere reminds me of the low point of mine. You were too young to remember, but I can't forget it. That awful day still hurts when I think of it and that piece of jewelry your father gave me always brings it back."

149

She began replacing everything into the safe-deposit box, everything except the small envelope which contained the nickel she had found in a popcorn ball fifty years before. "I want you to have this now," she said, smiling. "It's your legal fee for the day's work."

I didn't consider it work, and as it turned out Mama's disposition of her treasures wasn't a rough draft, either. That was the only will she ever made.

I wasn't too young to remember the day Mama referred to, the day she called the "low point" of her marriage. I even remember coming home at noontime for dinner as I did every day (we lived just two blocks from Washington School), walking in the back door and finding Mama in the kitchen, crying. She had taken Manny to the neighbor's and had telephoned my sisters' teachers that she was sending Beulah to the school with their dinners. I think she lied and said she was replastering the house. Mama was a firm believer that people are never satisfied until they hear what they want to hear. Our class had been dismissed a few minutes early that day and I was already on my way home when Mama tried to intercept me, so I walked in and found Mama crying in the kitchen and Papa screaming in the front part of the house.

"Your father's mad," she said, putting the food on my plate and making a place for me to eat at the kitchen table. "Real mad."

I could hear Papa hollering and complaining and although it was unpleasant it didn't bother me too much because I'd heard it before. Even the occasional sound of something being broken or banged around wasn't too unusual. There was almost a formula to it. First Papa would let out a bloodcurdling, Neanderthalic scream, then there would be a crash or a splintering. I am sure that Mama was such an authority on Papa's tantrums that she could tell from the intensity of the scream and the subsequent explosion whether what he was breaking was valuable or not.

"I don't think you'd better go out of the kitchen."

"All right, Mama."

"Can you wait until you're at school to go to the bathroom?"

"Yes, Mama."

But just then there was a loud crash involving glass that sounded ominous and Mama ran out of the kitchen to see what Papa had broken. Instead of staying where I was I followed her.

The house was a wreck. Chairs, tables and sofas were overturned, drapes and curtains lay in incongruous piles on the floor. Papa had snatched the scarves off dressers causing the atomizers, mirrors, pictures and dozens of other things that stayed on them to be scattered all over the room. Many lamps had been knocked over, their shades torn and bent and ruined.

As she rushed toward Papa Mama saw one of her cut-glass bowls in pieces on the hall floor. It shocked her so much she actually stopped for a second as though she wanted to pick up the pieces, to hold them in her hand. It was the only time Papa had ever broken anything that really "mattered" to her. No matter how mad he got Mama knew he would never touch her cut glass nor her silver nor her figurines nor the hand-painted plates that were displayed on the high dado which went around the walls of the dining room. Even in his most unreasonable rages there was a strange reasonableness about what he destroyed and what he considered off limits.

Papa looked dazed as he stood breathing hard in the middle of the parlor holding his right fist which was bleeding. He had rammed the fist through the big window that looked out on the driveway and pieces of glass were every place.

Mama picked up an organdy curtain and wrapped it around his hand. All she said was "Max . . ." Her tone of voice was half scold, half pity. Papa, whose eyes were still glazed with anger, was suddenly subdued from the painful crash. To Mama, it was apparent that the peak of his fury had been reached and from now on it would be downhill.

Mama ran to the telephone and called Dr. Longmire who had just finished his noon meal and hadn't yet begun his noontime nap. He told her to send Max over.

"I told Dr. Longmire you'd accidentally cut your hand while putting up a window," she said. "He's waiting to treat it."

Papa, still huffing and puffing, but almost docile, marched out the front door and across the street to the doctor's house with the blood-stained organdy curtain still wrapped around his hand.

"You can go to the bathroom now," Mama said to me. She had hoped she and Beulah could clean up the mess, but I'd already seen it and there was nothing to hide now.

Mama gave me a piece of chocolate cake to take to Mrs. Mauldin, my fourth-grade teacher. "It's going to be all right now," she said to me. "When Papa comes back from Dr. Longmire's I'll make him eat his dinner. He'll pout awhile but then he'll calm down." She automatically picked up a clean cup towel, wiped a corner of my mouth, and added, "Until next time."

I remember the scene so well because of what I asked Mama next and the way she answered me.

"What's Papa so mad about?"

"I'm not sure. His mother insists that he give her the first thousand dollars in royalties from each oil well so she can bring her relatives to this country. He's sent her fifteen thousand dollars already and a new well came in yesterday. He thinks I'm opposed to it and it makes him mad that I won't say so. I think *he's* opposed to it and this is his way of saying so. Or maybe it's something else entirely. He's going to New York tomorrow to buy for the store. Maybe that's the reason. He doesn't like to leave home because he buys too much and then he has to sweat to sell it all. It always starts from nothing, absolutely nothing. Today it was a button missing on his shirt. Something little like that sets him off and he builds up steam. Now he'll be sorry. And when he's in New York he'll buy me a present. And he'll be real sweet. Until next time."

"But Mama," I blurted out, "why do you let him?" And then I said something I'd be even sorrier for saying if I had been older at the time. It was a childish question, emanating from love or sympathy or both—but I wish I'd never spoken it: "Why don't you divorce Papa?"

Mama looked more stunned than she'd been when she saw the broken cut-glass bowl. She had to sit down at the kitchen table.

"What ever made you say *that?*" she asked, shakily.

"People get divorced when they get real mad like Papa is now, don't they?"

"Your father's not mad at *me*. He's mad at . . . *things*. He builds up and builds up and then he just has to explode. After that, he's wonderful." She put her hand on my cheek. "I couldn't divorce your papa because . . . I *love* him. And even if it doesn't look like it, he loves me, too." She said it again for emphasis. "He loves me very much. Now go to school and don't forget to give the piece of cake to Mrs. Mauldin."

Mama was right about the present. Papa went to Tiffany's and bought the flashy diamond lavaliere for her and gave it to her when he returned from market, together with the long letter he had written in that incredible handwriting. And while Papa was buying the present for her Mama was making a fruitcake for Dr. Longmire, who refused to send a bill for taking fourteen stitches in Papa's hand.

Mama had a weakness for peddlers. More accurately, she had a weakness for the exciting things peddlers sold. Where some women today are addicted to antique shops and spend a good deal of time going from one dealer to the other, in those days buyers stayed at home and antique shops came to them. Only one couldn't call the things that were bought and sold antiques. They were just pretty possessions: hooked rugs made by nuns in Canada, cloisonné bowls from China via San Francisco and New Orleans, carved wooden statuettes from India, fringed shawls, silver candelabra, and everything the O'Something sisters sold in the way of Irish linen and lace.

The O'Somethings spoke with a thick Irish brogue and always wrote a note telling Mama exactly what time they would ring our front doorbell. Mama always baked something special for them. The O'Somethings carried their own heavy bags, smiled a lot and loved to demonstrate to my sisters the way lace was made. They gave complimentary bobbins to people they liked and Mama and the girls had a whole drawerful of the pesky things.

It was puzzling how the peddlers found out about Mama.

They must have had a communications network that makes present-day walkie-talkies amateurish by comparison. Beulah insisted that the peddlers were like the tramps who streamed to our back door in search of food. She was certain that tramps had a mark which they left at a house where they had been given a handout. Of course you had to be a tramp before you knew where to look for such a mark because it was left in a tramp-secret place. "You cain't tell me they don't know which house is gonna feed 'em and which house is gonna turn 'em away. You won't catch a tramp askin' for somethin' to eat at you know who's (Beulah pointed toward the house she had in mind) because they's some kind of mark on *that* house that says plain as day Nothin' Doin'! Don't see no peddlers stoppin' there, neither."

Whether by word of mouth or by special signal, the peddlers knew that when the lady with the Southern accent on Oak Street in Sapulpa, Oklahoma, saw something she liked she bought it. The repeaters—the ones who came three or four times a year—respected Mama's taste and judgment. They knew she didn't like to haggle and sometimes passed over something she really wanted because she thought the price was too high. So they quoted their last price first and usually made the sale.

If Mama liked one peddler better than all the others (and she did) it would have to be Mr. Adwon. Mr. Adwon was in his early forties, was frail looking ("Is it any wonder? He just won't eat. I always offer him something but he won't eat a bite. He thanks me real sweet but says he's just eaten and he isn't hungry. Which I know for a fact isn't so"), had thick, heavily pomaded hair, unbelievably blue eyes, a speech impediment which added a note of incongruity to his difficult enough Near/Far Eastern accent, and a devastating smile for his customers whether or not they bought from him.

Mama considered Mr. Adwon a genius because it took him only one visit to learn that she liked small, beautiful things. Because she hid them as soon as they were hers he concluded that Papa did not like small, beautiful things. Without ever meeting Papa Mr. Adwon was positive that Papa didn't like peddlers either and he was right there, too. So Mr. Adwon was especially careful to pick a time when Papa was not at home. He might even have spied from a safe distance to be sure. He always parked his Buick touring car (with side curtains tightly fastened into place all the year) around the corner from our house.

Mama was busy in the kitchen when the doorbell rang so she sent Beulah to see who was there.

"It's Mr. Adwon," Beulah reported. "I just love that man. He always asks me how I'm feeling and how my children are doin'. Even if he don't mean a word of it it sure makes me feel good. I told him to sit down in the parlor and make himself at home."

"He means it," Mama said, crimping the dough around a pie plate and pouring in the apple filling. "Mr. Adwon's a gentleman. I've missed him. He hasn't been here since early May." She quickly braided the top crust dough, put the pie into the oven, took off her apron and hurried to the front of the house, smoothing her hair as she went.

Mr. Adwon sat on the edge of his chair in the shadowed room. When Mama walked in he shot up like one of his own jack-in-the-boxes and released a generous grin that showed all of his perfect white teeth.

"Meez Meyer, it be mos' fie month that I be here. You fee'in' good? Chil'ern fee'in' good?"

"We're all fine . . . and you look good, too." Mama spoke slowly and distinctly. She had no trouble understanding her friend. Some of his customers made a big thing of his strange jargon. Emily Smith liked to tell about the time she thought she was buying a damask tablecloth and napkin set only to learn that Mr. Adwon had been describing a car lap robe.

Mr. Adwon glanced quickly at the large black case on the floor near his chair but he said nothing. Protocol called for Mama to open the negotiations.

"Mr. Adwon, I'll tell you what I mainly want this time. Another cut-glass lamp. Like the one you sold me two years ago."

Mr. Adwon nodded his head to show that he remembered. "That one had sma faw."

"Yes. You told me it had a small flaw when you sold it to me. That's why I haven't felt too terribly bad that it got broken. Can you get me another?"

Mr. Adwon beamed. "Got one. Now. In wood box on for of car. Behin' driver seat. Zackly same lamp but no faw. I go get it."

"That isn't necessary. If you say it's the same lamp it's the same lamp. I always felt funny about the flaw in the other one even though nobody could see it without looking close. How much for this one?"

With Mama, Mr. Adwon didn't have to hesitate. "Sixty-fie dollar."

"I'll take it," Mama said. "And if you'll wait just a minute I'll get the money and pay you for it right now."

Mr. Adwon knew how Mama liked to deal. She preferred to pay for each item as she bought it. It was a strange way of doing business but there certainly was nothing wrong with it.

Mama liked to have cash where she could reach it in a hurry and she had a good deal of it stashed away in various parts of the house. Papa, who was a nut about secret hiding places, designed two or three of them especially for Mama. At the foot of one of his floor-to-ceiling mirrors was a long ornamental wooden baseboard which concealed a secret drawer at either end. In a small pantry off the kitchen Papa had constructed a very cleverly hidden chamber behind the beveled waist-high wooden wall that circled the room. By inserting the top of an ice pick into a microscopic hole in one of the grooves, that whole section lifted up and revealed an ample repository for a fairly large cache.

Mama's favorite hiding place, however, was in the bathroom. "Whoever looks in a bathroom for money?" Under the bottom shelf of the bathroom linen closet Papa had built a tiny drawer on wooden runners. By kneeling very low one could reach under the shelf and pull out the drawer. This is what Mama did now to get her sixty-five dollars for the new cut-glass lamp. She kept returning to the bathroom and getting down on her knees to tap the drawer for more cash for a cut-glass candy dish, which had a handsome six-inch stem and cut-glass base, and then again for money to pay for one of Mr. Adwon's luncheon set specials—a bridge-table-size cloth with four napkins—and still again for the purchase of a blue and gold bisque chocolate set on a bisque tray.

Each new possession was carefully put away before Mama looked at anything else. As it turned out, that was a good system because when Papa's Packard turned into the driveway Mama was in the clear. Mr. Adwon's bag was no problem. The problem was Mr. Adwon himself. If wouldn't do for Papa to find him in the parlor. It wouldn't do for Papa to find him *any*place. If Papa came in the front door she could sneak Mr. Adwon out the back. If Papa came in the back door she could sneak Mr. Adwon out the front. But what about the cut-glass lamp? It was hers now—even though it was in a box in Mr. Adwon's car.

She pushed the black case into a corner, then pushed Mr. Adwon down the hall, through the kitchen and everyday dining room, and then down the steps to the basement.

Mama spoke as quickly as she dared without losing Mr. Adwon along the way. "My husband has come home early. I will give him his dinner and when he goes I will come down and get you. Do you mind waiting down here?"

"Yes," Mr. Adwon said, smiling politely.

Mama knew what he meant. "We'll be right above you," she said. "Just sit down on that chair over by the ironing board and I'll call you."

"Caw me?"

Mama had no more time. "Wait here. *Wait!*" she commanded and ran back up the stairs to the kitchen.

Fortunately, Papa had chosen to come in through the front door and while he was in the bathroom Mama turned the fire up on the soup, put some lamb chops in the broiler, opened a jar of her black-eyed peas and started to mash potatoes. By the time Papa appeared she had briefed Beulah as to Mr. Adwon's whereabouts and was ready to sit down with Papa while Beulah served the meal.

If Mr. Adwon had stayed put, if he had sat quietly in the chair Mama had pointed to, if he had patiently waited for Papa to eat his dinner and leave, there would be no story to tell. But Mr. Adwon, first exhilarated by Mama's purchases, then deflated at being pushed through a strange house, down basement stairs, and ordered to "Wait!" in a semidark basement, got up from the rickety chair by the ironing board and decided to reconnoiter.

First, he ventured into the room where Mama stored her home-canned provisions. He stared unbelievingly at the shelves filled with jars of peaches, pears, strawberries, all kinds of fruits and jellies, piccalilli and chowchow, dill pickles, green beans, beets and even corn on the cob and he came perilously close to making the sign of the cross at what to him was a heavenly sight. A man whose business it was to bring things of beauty to people who appreciated them could be excused for genuflecting when he himself came face to face with unexpected works of art like Mama's canned goods.

Then he walked back into the main room of the basement and listened for a few moments to Papa who was talking and eating just over his head. A few steps away, in a corner of the room, he discovered an overhead shower and a toilet (which he was tempted to use but was too shy to do so).

Finally, he wandered down a narrow passage which ran from the ironing room deep into the midsection of the house and terminated in a circular furnace room whose furnace was seldom used but which was nonetheless dry and warm from the hot-water heater located there.

Did I say *dry* and warm? That small round room, hidden under the heart of the house, was potentially the wettest spot in town. A ten-gallon glass water jug filled to its neck with Mama's best grape wine nestled in a wooden cradle near the unused furnace. Instead of a cork, the bottle wore a heavy porcelain mug for a cap to let the gas escape while keeping the air out of the wine. Mama used this mug to sample the product whenever she inspected her project. Sometimes she would nudge the bottle gently just to tease the fermenting grapes. (Nudge, mind you, not agitate! Mama believed that a loving caress whenever one passed by the cradle helped to speed the fermentation.) Soon she would transfer the purplish blue liquid from this big jar to smaller bottles, which could be tightly corked and covered with sealing wax.

When Mr. Adwon pulled the overhead light chain a small incandescent bulb gave a cozy, yellow aura to the tiny round room. At this point he had explored everything there was to explore in the basement. He could either go back to the ironing board area and sit on the hard, rickety chair Mama had offered him, or he could . . .

He lifted the mug from the wine bottle and tipped the bottle in its cradle ever so gently so that a bit of the clear liquid on top poured into the cup. He took a small sip of the wine, expecting a sharp, overly sour vintage. He had underestimated Mama. She was famous for the bouquet, the quality, the clearness, the lightness, the buoyancy, the delicious tastiness, and the wallop of her homemade grape wine. Mr. Adwon blinked his eyes, cocked his head as though he was listening to celestial music from a thousand harps, ran his tongue over his lips a time or two and immediately filled the mug to the brim with the wine.

Mr. Adwon was hungry and thirsty and the sweet liquid satisfied both cravings. Ten minutes later he started his second cupful. The more he drank the better it tasted. By the time he had finished his refill he felt a beauteous glow. He also felt the need to use the facilities—*any* facilities—before he burst. He actually toyed with the idea of opening the door to the furnace but decided against that (Mama was right: He *was* a gentleman) and marched manfully back to the front part of the basement and rediscovered the toilet just in time. Half conscious of his secret status he tried to make as little noise as possible by aiming at the upper part of the bowl above the water line but, thanks to his un-steadiness, he only partially succeeded. When he had finished he flushed the toilet, a simple, automatic gesture that almost caused Mama upstairs to have heart failure.

Papa was noisily sucking away at an almost-clean lamb chop when he heard the flush. He looked at Mama in a puzzled way and asked, "Who's downstairs?"

"Beulah's Sister is doing some ironing," Mama lied, hoping Mr. Adwon would not find it necessary to repeat the act. "Eat, honey," she said, piling Papa's plate with more whipped potatoes and black-eyed peas.

Mr. Adwon, who was feeling much more relaxed now, wended his way back down the narrow passageway to the little room that had won his heart. Recklessly tipping the bottle in its cradle so that sediment flared up from the bottom he slopped out another mugful of wine. If it was not as clear as his other samplings he either didn't know or didn't care because he gulped it down greedily and poured out still more, overtipping the bottle this time so that some of the wine overshot the cup and landed on his trouser legs and shoes. Mr. Adwon sat on the floor with his back braced against the furnace and began to sing. It was a weird sing-ing—more a wail than a song—with frequent catches in his throat that might have been sobs. Fortunately, he was far enough back into the basement to muffle most of the sound. But not all of it.

Papa's mouth was full of apple pie as he asked, "What the hell is that?"

"Beulah's Sister sings those sad spirituals," Mama said. "Should I open the basement door and ask her to stop?"

"Oh, leave her alone," Papa said, getting up from the table. "I've got to go pick up my Indians and take them out to the ranch. Ernie needs help on some stonework he's doing."

Mr. Adwon yipped another phrase or two.

"My God!" Papa said. "Call that *singing?* Sounds more like she's speaking in tongues."

"It does at that," Mama said, holding the back door open for Papa.

"Sorry, Annie. I've got to go out the front door. That's the way I came in."

"Oh, sure," Mama said, trying to hurry him through the house and out of it without actually pushing him. When she saw Beulah she dropped a step behind Papa and made an elaborate gesture, pointing first at the basement and then at Beulah to tell her to go there at once and release Mr. Adwon.

As soon as the front door was closed Mama streaked through the house like a thoroughbred in the home stretch and headed for the basement door. When she got there she found Beulah still upstairs, standing by the door with her arms folded.

"Haven't you seen him yet?" Mama asked. "Didn't you get my signal to go down there and tell Mr. Adwon he could come up now?"

"I got the signal," Beulah replied firmly. "But I'm not about to go down those steps while a man's taking a shower!"

"*What?*" Mama thought Beulah had lost her mind.

"Listen!" Beulah said.

Sure enough, one could hear the shower running. One could also hear an occasional snort from Mr. Adwon.

Mama wouldn't ask Beulah to do something that offended her sense of decency, so Mama herself opened the basement door and started cautiously down the stairs. Before she had descended far enough to look around she yelled, "Mr. Adwon! Are you okay?"

"Okay!" Mr. Adwon yelled back but he continued to splash under the shower.

Finally Mama looked.

Mr. Adwon was fully clothed. The water was peppering down on his head and running off his soaked suit. When he saw Mama he grinned at her and waved in a kind of salute.

Using an unironed tablecloth as a raincoat, Mama rushed over to the shower and turned it off. She called to Beulah to go to Papa's bedroom and get socks, underwear, a shirt and a pair of pants and bring them to the basement.

She and Beulah helped take off Mr. Adwon's suit coat, shirt, necktie and shoes, then shooed him into the canned-goods room for him to change the rest of his clothes himself. His protests made no difference because the two women simply overpowered him.

When Mr. Adwon reappeared he looked like a man who had suddenly shrunk while his clothes remained the same. Papa's pants were at least twelve sizes too large for him so Mama used a safety pin to hold them up and then folded back the overlap, tying it into place with an old bathrobe cord that served as a belt. She snickered every time she thought of Papa's size 52 BVDs under Mr. Adwon's pants and shirt.

Mr. Adwon started back toward the furnace room as though to retrieve something he had left there. Mama caught up with him, swung him around, and aimed him toward the steps.

"At least you're *dry*," she said as they slowly made their way upstairs. Mr. Adwon's wet shoes squished every time he took a step.

"Dwi?" he asked, weakly.

"Sit there!" she said, pointing to Papa's place at the dining-room table. "You're going to eat a bowl of soup. Don't tell me that you've just eaten because I know you haven't."

Mr. Adwon obliged. In fact, he ate two bowlfuls, tearing up pieces of Mama's homemade bread and floating them in each.

Beulah squeezed the water out of Mr. Adwon's soaked clothes and then wrapped them in a towel. His wallet, fat with Mama's recent purchase money, was relatively dry. Mama decided against putting it into one of the overlapping pockets of Papa's pants . . . so she placed it in Mr. Adwon's black suitcase and told him three times where she had put it. Even so, she made him open the suitcase and point to the wallet just to be certain he did remember.

"Now we're going to walk you to your car so I can get my cut-glass lamp."

"Ol' lamp had sma faw. It boke."

"Yes, the old one is broken," Mama said, happy that Mr. Adwon was at last coming back to his senses. "You sold me the lamp you have in your car which has no flaw at all. Remember?"

Mr. Adwon nodded.

Fortunately, there was no traffic on Oak Street at three o'clock on that mild late-September afternoon when Mama and Beulah escorted Mr. Adwon out of the house to the corner, then to his car a half block up the street in the other direction. Beulah carried the bundle of clothes, Mama carried the black suitcase, and both half-carried Mr. Adwon who looked like a scarecrow in Papa's clothes. The shirttails of the size-19 shirt bulged unevenly from where they were stuffed into the cavernous trousers. The shoes still squished but at least Mr. Adwon was walking fairly straight in them by the time they reached the car.

Beulah spread the wet clothes over the back seat so they would dry more quickly. Mama found the wooden crate with her lamp in it exactly where Mr. Adwon said it was. The black suitcase was placed on the front seat by Mr. Adwon's side and on top of it Mama placed a chicken sandwich wrapped in wax paper.

"Good-bye, Mr. Adwon," Mama said. "We'll see you on your next trip."

Mr. Adwon didn't answer. With sobriety had come remorse.

"Okay?" Mama asked brightly.

"Okay," Mr. Adwon answered, but his heart wasn't in it. For a few seconds it was touch and go as to whether he would actually break down and cry.

"Now don't you feel bad, Mr. Adwon," Beulah volunteered. "We're your friends. Nobody's perfect."

"Beulah's right," Mama added. "Nobody's perfect. All of us are like that broken lamp. We all have our flaws."

"Sma faws." As Mr. Adwon said it he offered a watered-down version of his sweet smile and twinkled his blue eyes just a little bit. Mama and Beulah knew he was all right then.

When they got back to the house they carefully opened the wooden crate and removed the cut-glass lamp, which was as perfect as Mr. Adwon had promised it would be. Mama showed Beulah everything else she had bought that day. Then the two of them went into the kitchen where Mama whipped up a devil's food cake while Beulah washed the dinner dishes. They each drank a glass of homemade grape wine to settle their nerves.

Mama had her faults, but cutting people down wasn't one of them. She only lost her patience with people who used power or position to downgrade others. And yet, I remember one scene she played in which she pulled her rank for all it was worth.

The Great Lady Act took place in Neiman-Marcus, a store Mama wasn't overly fond of because of Aunt Mabel's love-hate relationship to it.

All of us (except Papa, of course) had driven to Taro for a short visit. It was a relaxed trip because Mama didn't have to ask Uncle Ed for money this time. The oil wells on the ranch were still flowing enough to enable Papa to buy the pieces of land that adjoined what he already owned and to build such necessary improvements as a barbecue pit, bull-sized, onto the dance pavilion, a natural-stone setting around the flagpole, and individual wood-burning fireplaces in the houses of his tourist court.

The trip was my sister Pearl's idea. She had received a new car as a high school graduation present and this was a chance to show it off. Mama and Papa had put their heads together and decided that if Pearl had a car of her own she wouldn't be so apt to run away and get married as her sister, Bea, had done. I felt like telling them they were goofy because a car would only make it easier to elope in but I kept my mouth shut. There was always the hope that Pearl might let me drive her car after the newness wore off.

It was a bright red Chrysler 66 convertible with that greatest car gimmick of the century, a rumble seat. The rumble seat was located in what today is the trunk. A gentle tug on the outside handle and a leather-upholstered extra seat pulled up. You got into it from the outside by placing your foot on a special step near the back fender and climbing in. It was an open-cockpit type of operation but it was fun to ride back there in splendid isolation. Inevitably, the rumble seat will make a comeback. When it does, people will refer to it as a jump seat or a mother-in-law seat as they did forty years ago. My brother and I sat in the rumble seat of Pearl's car all the way from Sapulpa to Taro and back. One experience like that and a man can truly say he has communed with nature.

It was exciting seeing Emma and Varney and all the aunts, uncles and cousins again. Uncle Ed was so relieved to learn that Mama was not after a handout that he gave her a check for $500. But after a week of reunioning Mama began her usual fidgeting for home and we started back in Pearl's car.

The stores were just opening for business when we arrived in Dallas, and since we were driving through the business section of the city Mama said suddenly, "Pearl, dear. Would you mind driving around the block while Lewis and I run into Neiman's? Mabel has her heart set on a cake plate but they won't sell it to her because they know she'll send it back. I'd like to buy it and send it to her for a gift."

"But, Mama! You don't look nice enough to go into Neiman's," Pearl said.

"Don't be silly. We're tourists and tourists always dress . . . informally."

I jumped out of the rumble seat, Manny climbed up front with his sister and Mama and I entered Neiman-Marcus, the first customers of the day.

The employees were still dusting and straightening stock when we arrived on the floor where the cake plate was. They glanced at us but not one of them made the slightest effort to ask if we wanted anything.

In all fairness to the institution that Neiman-Marcus was

then let me say that neither Mama nor I conformed to the image of the typical Neiman-Marcus customer. Mama wore a scarf on her head (the color and material of it made one think of Papa's famous puce pongee collarless shirts and that scarf may well have been a faded remnant of one of them), a white blouse she had elected to wear over her cotton skirt instead of tucking it inside, stockings that she had rolled down to her kneecaps for coolness, and tennis shoes. I wore a short-sleeved sport shirt with a tear on the right sleeve, white duck pants, and sandals that had thin strips of leather plaited on them like an openwork design on a peach cobbler. You might say we were straws in the wind of what was destined to be known as the Okie image.

"You'd think that one of those clerks would ask us what we want," Mama said to me. "Pearl's driving around and around the block and I can't find Mabel's cake plate in all this clutter."

Now that I reconstruct the scene I can see how the salespeople thought we were part of the pre-store-hours' cleaning force.

Finally, Mama marched up to a woman who had been pointedly ignoring us and said, "I'm trying to find a cake plate."

The woman looked us up and looked us down. Her reserve collapsed completely when she encountered Mama's tennis shoes. "You must have the wrong store," she said in a voice cool enough to frost the whole floor. "*This* is Neiman-Marcus!"

The way she said it infuriated Mama. All the suppressed animosity toward this store that spurned her sister Mabel's love for it by discouraging all purchases began to bubble and boil inside her.

There was a telephone on a cashier's desk nearby and Mama walked briskly to it as though she dispatched messages on that phone every day of her life. While she was waiting for the operator to answer Mama was frantically trying to recall which owner Mabel had said was "in the family": Mr. Neiman . . . or Mr. Marcus? *Eeny meeny, miney mo* . . . She did remember his first name, however, so when the operator asked her what she wanted Mama answered in a ringing voice that even her brother Julius would envy, "Stanley's office, please!"

"Stanley *Marcus?*" the operator must have said.

"Who else?" Mama answered, gaining momentum.

I don't know what answer Mama got, if any, but she gave the operator a crisp, "Thank you," replaced the earpiece and set the phone back on the counter.

"Stanley hasn't come in yet," she said to no one in particular. Then, to the discourteous saleslady, she said, "He's in the family. Now may I see the cake plates?"

The First Lady of the Land wouldn't have rated more attention than Mama got with those cake plates. It didn't take her a minute to find the one Mabel wanted and even though the saleswoman insisted that she charge it—her only way of knowing who this woman was!—Mama insisted on paying cash.

We'd learned one thing about Mama. When we were with her we never had to worry about running out of money because she always carried plenty. Papa, on the other hand, took a delight in never having fifty cents in his pockets. He gloried in appearing to be dead broke because he knew that if worst came to worst he could raise any amount he needed simply by speaking up. Not Mama. She always had enough cash with her to make a down payment on a house. She didn't often need it, but she had it if she wanted it.

As we walked toward the elevator Mama paused at a display of cut glass built around an enormous cut-glass punch bowl. Mama actually trembled with excitement the moment she saw it. She'd begged Mr. Adwon to find her one but he'd had no luck. And here it was. Exactly what she'd known a cut-glass punch bowl would look like, even to the silver ladle inside it. As anxious as I was to continue the trip home I remember turning away and pretending to be interested in something else so Mama could indulge herself in the luxury of staring at that bowl.

In the background, huddled together like the witches in *Macbeth*, the crones who worked in the gift department were being filled in by our erstwhile saleslady. I caught the words "Stanley Marcus" and "in her family" and "*tennis* shoes!" The general idea seemed to be that Mama was very rich and therefore could be as eccentric as she chose to be.

Mama ran her hands over the grooves of the cut-glass bowl, lifted the ladle to serve an imaginary cup of her own legendary eggnog and then lovingly placed her two hands around the base of the bowl and lifted it from the table to feel its weight.

One of the crones dashed toward Mama with surprising agility, moving her hips like a hula dancer as she wove in and out of the display tables. "Be very careful with that punch bowl," she admonished breathily. "It's expensive. Maybe you'd better put it back on the table where you found it."

"How expensive?" Mama asked, not taking her eyes off it and making no move to set it down.

"*Three hundred dollars!*" the crone replied, reaching for the bowl.

"I'll take it," Mama said. Then, turning to me, she said, "I'll go down and find Pearl. It'll make her nervous if she has to go around the block many more times. Give this (she handed me three hundred-dollar bills) to the cashier over yonder and tell her to pack the bowl in lots of tissue paper so it won't break."

Without looking at the flabbergasted saleswoman, Mama punched the mother-of-pearl button, got into the elevator and disappeared. Seeing her that way was a new and strange experience for me. She didn't act like Mama at all. She acted like a duchess in tennis shoes.

7. "My Wrists Are Weak"

"My wrists are weak," Mama complained to Mrs. Longmire as the two of them stood in the Longmire front yard assessing the damage done by the family Reo when it jumped the curb and plowed into the Longmire magnolia tree. The Reo had momentum but the magnolia was older and stouter and the tree had won.

"It's always the same," Mama said, after apologizing for the car tracks across the Longmire lawn and the badly skinned tree. "My wrists suddenly lose their strength and I can't hold a car in the street." She wriggled her wrists experimentally. "I'm not going to try it again right now. I'll send one of the children to drive the Reo home. Max's Indians will start work on your yard first thing in the morning."

Mrs. Longmire said she was thankful nobody was hurt and urged Mama not to worry about the yard. Like the other neighbors up and down Oak Street who were veterans of Mama's curb jumping, Mrs. Longmire was gracious about the whole thing. If Mama had weak wrists she was strong in other ways. "She does many good deeds," was the reply wives gave their husbands who wanted to know why everybody was so nice to a woman who preferred driving on their front yards to driving in the street.

Mama had been expressing her affinity for front yards ever since Papa had bought the Chandler many years earlier. She had tried to drive the Oakland, then the Hupmobile, but both attempts had ended in front yard disasters. Sometimes months would go by before she'd try again. She actually broke a wheel off the Hupmobile when she jumped the curb and hit an old cement hitching post instead of the usual soft dirt and grass. Once, when she smashed into a tree with the Franklin, Ernie Cooper, who was sitting in the front seat with her, said, "Don't worry about smashing the radiator, Mrs. Meyer. The Franklin is air cooled so there ain't no radiator to smash." He thought for a moment and added, helpfully, "Mebbe you oughtta drive the Franklin all the time!"

While she never tackled Papa's Packard Twin Six she did take a tree with her the time she drove/rode my Dodge Business Coupe through the Briscoe yard. The lovely Jennings rose garden was never the same after Mama's invasion of it with a short-lived Oldsmobile.

She made her last foray into the greenery in the same Reo with which she had assaulted the Longmire magnolia. She had started for the Safeway store to get some hamburger meat for dinner when she found herself in the Croston yard decapitating their prize azalea and chipping the bricks off that corner of the house where the bush had been. Mrs. Croston was just as sweet as Mrs. Longmire had been and the Croston boy drove the Reo home and parked it on our driveway. Mama walked.

Papa was waiting for her.

"Hello, Max," she began. "It's these wrists again—they're weak."

Papa couldn't bear the thought of one of his loved ones having weak anythings so he tried to argue Mama out of her notion.

"It's all in your mind," he said, with all the tact of a bulldozer.

"My mind?"

"Yes. You make up your mind before you start that you can't steer a car and sure enough that's the way it works out. Honey-darling, forget that weak-wrist business and say loudly, 'I can drive a car!'"

Mama looked at him.

"Damn it, Annie. *Say* it!"

"Say what?"

"Say, 'I can drive a car!'" He shook his head. "Not *me. You!* Repeat these words after me: I CAN DRIVE A CAR!"

Mama, miserable at being a party to Papa's inquisition, repeated the words, "I can drive a car."

"Of course you can!" Papa exulted, putting his bear arms around her and lifting her off her feet. "You can *do* it, Annie!" he shouted, kissing her on the mouth with a loud smack. "Now come to the car with me and *prove* it!"

"Not right now, Max. Later."

"No time like the present! I'll sit by your side in the front seat."

"My God, no!"

He started pulling Mama by her hand toward the driveway. "Nothing to be afraid of." If her wrist had been weak earlier it was helpless by the time he had her there.

Papa's Packard was on the driveway close to the garage so he chose the Reo which was parked behind it. Like

175

pushing someone back into the water after he has almost drowned, Papa figured Mama would get more good out of her driving lesson if she used the same car she had just grounded.

Gallantly, Papa opened the door of the sporty green car and half-helped, half-pushed Mama behind the wheel. Then he closed the door, walked quickly around the car and got in beside her.

"Here we go!" he said in the same pseudocheerful voice he used to encourage us to drink our Epsom salts or stuff Mentholatum up our noses.

Mama had had a half-dozen driving teachers but not one of them made her tremble the way Max did now. She turned the key in the ignition switch and put her foot on the starter. The engine responded.

"See, Annie? You can start a car as well as any driver in the world!" He craned his head around. "Nothing coming either way. Shift gears, step on the gas and back 'er up!"

It happened so quickly Papa couldn't do a thing to prevent it. Mama shifted gears all right, but in her confusion she shifted to forward instead of reverse. She also stepped on the gas as Papa had urged her to. Before Papa could do anything except scream in anguish Mama had knocked the hell out of the rear of his car with the front of hers.

Mama jumped out of the car and stood on the grass by the driveway looking at the Reo's nose nudging the bruised rear end of the Packard and she began to cry.

Papa ran around the car, started the engine and slowly backed it away from the Packard.

"No harm done!" he said, making a Herculean effort to be sweet. "No harm—" He started to repeat the words but when he saw the Reo's crumpled head lamp and the Packard's broken bumper and bent fender he couldn't finish.

He walked over to Mama and put his arm around her. "Don't cry, honey-darling. I still say it's all in your mind. The children have been driving since they were twelve. Ernie Cooper drives when he's so drunk he can't see. Your friends in the Shakespeare Club drive their own cars. Even those idiot Levys in Taro drive. And *you can drive, too*—if you stop crying like a baby and *try.*"

Mama, who seemed so tiny by comparison, melted into him as she put her head on his chest and kept on crying like a baby.

"It's just something I can't do, Max," she said, reaching into his pants pocket for his handkerchief and using it to wipe her eyes and blow her nose. "Some people never learn how to swim, and that's the way I am about cars. I just can't learn to drive." She remembered the hamburger meat that had started it all. "Will you drive me to Safeway now?"

Papa sighed, got into the Reo, waited, ungallantly, while Mama got into the front seat by herself, then drove her to the grocery store. When they returned to the house he carried the groceries into the kitchen, sat down at the kitchen table, and visited with Mama while she began to put a white cake together. When she started her spirited stirring of the cake batter he stopped talking and stared at her.

The silence puzzled her. Mama stopped her stirring and asked, "What's the matter, Max?"

"Your wrists, Annie. I've been studying your wrists. Anyone who can beat a batter with all that strength can't have weak wrists."

Mama looked first at her wrists, then at the batter, then at Papa.

"Annie, you don't have to drive a car if you don't want to but there's one thing for sure: Your wrists ain't weak." He got up, walked over to her and patted her affectionately. "Honey, promise me you won't tell anybody else you have weak wrists. Your wrists are just fine."

Mama gave the batter a final whip, then poured it into the cake pan. Then she looked at Papa and grinned for the first time that day. "Maybe you're right, Max. My wrists ain't weak."

He beamed at her.

"It's my mind."

After that, whenever Mama wanted to go someplace one of us drove her, and by the process of elimination the job of being the driver fell more and more to me. On my thirteenth birthday Papa gave me a car of my own, and while he didn't pin me down to any bargain, it was tacitly understood that before I scooted off on my own I was to check first to see if Mama wanted to be driven anywhere.

I drove. I knew where every member of the Shakespeare Club lived and Mama and I often picked up two or three of the Shakespeare members and took them to the meeting with us. Mama bragged about me a lot and called me her personal chauffeur and I took pride in filling the part. I drove her to get her groceries, drove her to the post office where she took care of private business, mostly at the postal savings window ("A personal chauffeur always keeps his mouth shut"), hauled clothes and food and even furniture to the Salvation Army Hut, and at Mama's request I drove Major Miller to the dentist's in Tulsa every Friday afternoon until all his teeth were pulled and his bridge finished. I drove Mama to St. Louis several times to visit Bea, once to Taro when Varney died, and once to Hot Springs, Arkansas, during the racing season.

The Good Old Days were good in so many ways. Most of the restrictions that hem us in today didn't even exist. People weren't yet computer punch cards, the calendar wasn't a reminder of withholding tax due dates, and when it came to driving a car it was every man for himself. There were no drivers' licenses, no parking meters, no age qualifications, no red-and-green traffic lights, few if any stop signs, no fences to keep cows and horses from wandering onto the road, not even a white line down the middle of the highway. There are valid reasons for these things today . . . and the very thought of thirteen-year-olds driving their own cars is enough to make the modern driver (and pedestrian) shudder. But even in the Good Old Days there were some things that were taboo. One of them was weaving in and out of neighbors' front yards. Since Mama was an incorrigible weaver she was forced to become a passenger so she left the driving to me.

We offered to take Pearl to the races with us but she didn't want to go. Manny wanted to go but couldn't because he was too young to be admitted to the race track. Papa couldn't go with us because he, Ernie and his Indians were in the midst of their latest project: scooping out dirt to form an island at the shallow end of the lake.

So Mama and I drove to Hot Springs in the new seven-passenger Cadillac Papa had bought in Cleveland, Ohio, the summer before, after he had fallen asleep at the wheel of the old one and wrecked it. From a distance, the bright red car with its Oklahoma license plates and striped Indian blanket draped over the front seat might have belonged to a young Osage, traveling with his Indian mother. Even at closer

179

range, Mama's long black hair, only partially hidden by a red silk scarf, preserved the tribal illusion.

I was unable to put my finger on the motive for the Hot Springs trip. Ostensibly, the races themselves were reason enough, but Mama had never been to a race track so there couldn't have been a tug from that quarter. She certainly had no burning desire to see Papa's sister or brother who lived within spitting distance of each other (and never lacked for saliva).

Papa's father and mother had been dead for several years, and while Mama was pleasant enough to her remaining Hot Springs in-laws it took an effort on her part to smile at them. Sure enough, I saw Mama's smile disappear as soon as my aunt's and uncle's front doors had closed behind us.

"They look at us funny," I said, starting the car.

"I guess we look at them funny, too," Mama said.

We were slowly driving back to the hotel. "Something's goofy, Mama. Aunt Mabel, Uncle Sam, Uncle Julius and all the Taro people are more like . . . well, like *relatives*. This aunt and this uncle seem like . . . well, like *people* instead of kinfolks."

"Maybe it's my fault that you don't know your father's family better," Mama conceded. "But I don't think so. Your father himself doesn't know them. Or maybe he knows them too well. After what happened I can't say I blame him for feeling hurt."

"Just exactly what did happen?" If I was old enough to drive her on an overland trip I was old enough for Mama to tell me some of the shushed-up parts of our family history.

"They treated Max like a black sheep. Your grandfather left his land and buildings and money to all the others. He left five dollars to your father. I never learned why he did it—and if your father knew the reason he never told me." She smiled grimly. "Max never even got the five dollars."

She didn't know whether to stop or keep going. "I never understood your grandmother. Max was a good son and I tried to be a good daughter-in-law. We really tried, but somehow we both failed. She refused to come to visit us. She wouldn't even come when each of your sisters graduated from high school. You'd think the first thousand dollars from each oil well would have made her feel kindlier to us. Less, if anything."

"Maybe the Hot Springs relatives thought we didn't need anything with the oil and all."

"Everybody needs something. Not money, necessarily. But fair play. It wasn't right for your grandfather to cut your father out without at least an explanation. It hurt Max more than anything in his whole life hurt him."

Once launched, Mama revealed things she had kept to herself all these years. "It all points to me," she said without vindictiveness. "The Hot Springs people never forgave Max for marrying me. They thought the Levys were snobs. Maybe we were. *I* don't think so, but maybe we were. Snobs or not, we Levys have always had a kind of family feeling—the closeness you were talking about. It hurts sometimes almost as much as it helps but it's there and it's important. My own father changed his will when Max did that crazy-fool thing with the safe. He was afraid of Max so he fixed it so Max couldn't spend Levy money. But he was fair. He built the store building for us in Sapulpa and he made it plain that what was mine would belong to my children so I still got my part. But to cut your own child off, your own flesh and blood . . ." It was an effort for her to keep from crying. "To make him look like a criminal. To hurt him as they hurt your father. That wasn't right."

We were driving down Bathhouse Row and Mama said suddenly, "Stop the car over there."

"Where?"

"There. In front of that bathhouse. The one marked Quapaw."

I stopped.

"It was right there . . . *right there* . . . that I met your father. Come out of the car and I'll show you."

"I don't think I'd better get out here on Central Avenue," I said.

"Oh, come on. They wouldn't arrest a tourist for stopping to pay tribute to a landmark."

Landmark? We got out of the car and Mama walked to a spot on the sidewalk directly in front of the Quapaw Bathhouse and said almost clinically, "Here. Right here is where I first saw Max Meyer. My family were all here for the baths. We were all walking in this direction from the Arlington Hotel, and Max was walking toward us all by himself. . . . I think he was whistling. . . . And, well, it was precisely at this square of the sidewalk that we met." If she'd had a bucket of paint she would have X'd the spot.

Even after we had resumed driving Mama kept looking back at the Quapaw Bathhouse. "It looked exactly the same," she said, unbelievingly. "The same forsythia was in full bloom . . . and the same flowering peach. The grass was as green as it is now, and just as neat and pretty. . . . Yes, Max *was* whistling, because my father got mad. He insisted Max was whistling at *me*." All the sadness was gone from her eyes. "And now that I think about it, he was right!"

If there had to be a motive for our Hot Springs trip, this

was it. The past had pulled Mama here. And when she would return home again she would report to the man who had whistled at her all those years ago that the place where they had met was exactly as it had been. Looking at her now it was obvious that the thrill was the same, too.

Not many horseplayers can remember their first day at a race track, but I remember mine. I was fourteen years old, I was accompanied by my mother, and I won.

It was plainly Mama's first trip, too, because she couldn't answer any of the questions I asked. We sat quietly in the Oaklawn Park grandstand getting the feel of the place while the first two races were run. The noise and screams and willy-nilly rushing around confused us. Then Mama went to the Ladies Room and when she returned she acted excited.

"I know which horse is going to win the third race," she said. "The ladies in the rest room told me."

"How do they know?" I asked.

"They *know*," Mama said. "There are half a dozen of them and they come here every day and sit in the same chairs all afternoon inside the door of the Ladies Room and they pick their winners right there." She handed me four dollars. "There's two dollars for you and two dollars for me. Go to the window and tell the man the number of the horse you want and give him two dollars for the bet. I want Number 3."

"Number 3?"

"Yes, that's the one the ladies said to bet on. Number 3 in the third race. Hurry."

I was back within two minutes.

"That was quick. Did you bet Number 3?"

"I didn't bet anything. The man at the window asked me how old I was and I told him I was fourteen and he said,

'Jesus Christ! Go back to school!' You're supposed to be eighteen, Mama."

Mama took the four dollars, walked up to the first window she saw, bought two tickets on Number 3 and handed me mine as soon as she returned to her seat.

We hadn't bought a program so we had no idea what the Number 3 horse was called but we could see his number even if we didn't know his name, and when they started running the Number 3 horse was ahead all the way. The ladies in the rest room were right. Number 3 won and Mama and I each got back $18 for our $2 bet.

Mama left immediately for the Ladies Room and was gone quite a while. "They took a long time to make up their minds," she apologized. "They finally took a vote and the majority picked Number 6."

Of course Number 6 won. Mama and I each had won $12 more.

"There's really not much to it, is there?" she said to me. "I've concluded that you just have to find out which horse is going to win and bet on that one."

As I look back on a misspent life at handicapping I can honestly say that Mama's conclusion was the understatement of all time.

Mama looked puzzled when she came back from the Ladies Room before the next race.

"Who do they pick?" I asked.

"They don't pick any of them," she said. "They told me they weren't betting on this one and advised me not to bet, either." She showed me a ticket. "I didn't bet anything for you . . . but I bet for me. I bet Number 9. Our post-office box at home is Number 27, and 2 and 7 are 9 so I bet two dollars on Number 9."

Word gets out—and by this time the people sitting near us were aware of the small woman with the Texas accent who had picked two winners in a row. They were appalled when Mama told them she had now picked Number 9, a 60-to-1 shot. When Number 9 won they were dumbfounded.

"Lady, you've just won yourself $120," the man next to Mama said to her.

Mama was delirious with joy. She kept jumping up and down and then she announced she was going to get her winnings and report her luck to the rest-room ladies.

Time went by, and when Mama didn't come back for the next race I began to get worried. Maybe the excitement had made her sick? Maybe the ladies in the rest room had taken her money away from her? Or worse yet, maybe she had joined their sorority and would spend her remaining afternoons in the race track Ladies Room betting the horses?

When she finally did return she wasn't excited any more. She was literally shaking with anger. "They cheated me," she announced coldly.

"How, Mama?"

"I took my ticket to the man and told him to give me my $120. He admitted my horse had won $120 but he said I had bought a show ticket, whatever that is, and all I had won was $12.80. I made him go over it several times and the line behind me got longer and longer and he finally told me if I had a complaint I should go to the manager of the race track. I did, of course, and it didn't do one bit of good. All they would give me was $12.80."

The rest-room ladies had neglected to tell Mama about win, place and show. To Mama, a $2 bet was a $2 bet. She'd been lucky and bought her tickets at the win window the other times. This time the law of averages had caught up with her.

I wish I could say that Mama was a good sport about the payoff and was always careful to place her bets at the win window from that race on. After all, she was winner for the day and so was I. The truth is that Mama never bet another horse as long as she lived.

"Let's go," she said. "I don't like this place."

I didn't argue with her. After all, I couldn't bet without her.

"Can I keep what I won, Mama?" I asked on the way out.

"It's yours to do what you want to with," Mama said. "I'm giving what I won to the Salvation Army as soon as we get home. That's the only way to take the taint off."

Mama was through with racing forever. The people didn't play fair. When you won big money they cheated you out of it. No amount of reasoning could ever change her.

I was more forgiving of the track people. In fact, I returned every chance I got and by the time I was old enough to place a bet on my own I was a capital-H Horseplayer. Like a million others, I've had a few good days . . . and more than a few bad ones. Even before the dust from the last race has settled you'll find me scanning tomorrow's entries in an effort to recoup. Years have gone by. The hundreds of days and the thousands of horses have a way of fading, one into the other. But that first day at the race track, with Mama making the bets, is still fresh. I think of her whenever a longshot Number 9 comes home. And I marvel that she could quit when she did—the only race track bettor in history who could honestly say she never picked a loser! But Mama enjoyed an advantage that I would never have. She got her tips in the Ladies Room.

During the month of December when I wasn't driving Mama she was driving me. As soon as she had fed me my after-school snack she enlisted my services for intensive shopping expeditions. I merely steered; Mama drove. Sapulpa High School let out (that's the expression people used: "let out") a full week before Christmas and from that moment I became her full-time personal chauffeur.

Christmas was an almost unbearably complicated time for Mama. Naturally she bought presents for our family, her Texas people, and the friends and neighbors. But each member of the Salvation Army got something, too—something, as she put it, "he would never buy for himself." Once I made three trips to the music store in Tulsa just to get special arrangements of hymns for Mama to give Major Miller. That was the year she looked every place for a curling iron set for Marian Miller and ended up buying it from a mail-order house in Chicago. The Bledsoes' son Billy always got a book and his younger brother, Jerry, always got a game or toy. It was important to Mama that Billy's book be a superbook and Jerry's gift a supergame or supertoy, nicer than anything anyone else in school received. Then there were the ladies of the Shakespeare Club—each one of them had to be "matched up"—and all our teachers (not just the current ones; some on Mama's list went back to the first grade) and every member of Beulah's family and every member of Beulah's Sister's family and every person who worked in the store all the years we had it. Plus Ernie and Kate Cooper and all the families who lived on WPA Row. The postman got a necktie, the newspaper boy got candy, the boy who delivered groceries when Mama ordered by telephone got a shirt. She even sent her own whiskied fruitcakes to Mr. Adwon and the O'Something sisters. Christmastime, to Mama, was the time when you remembered everyone you knew, and not just with a card or note—but with a present. "Something personal" was the way she expressed it.

As though choosing and buying the presents wasn't enough of a challenge Mama had the additional problem of keeping her Christmas maneuvering out of Papa's orbit.

"What he doesn't know won't hurt him," Mama said.

"You mean, what he doesn't know won't gum up the works," I corrected.

Looking back on it, if Papa had guessed the extent to which Mama outdid the Three Wise Men in the gift department he would have gone up in smoke.

As much as Mama adored Christmas, every phase of it, Papa tried to ignore it. He was too polite to criticize, and so long as he was in business he felt he had no right to say anything against a season he, along with everybody else, profited from.

It was only after he had staged one final "Good-bye Forever! Going Out of Business Once and for All Sale" and then rented his building to the Safeway people for a second Sapulpa store that he spoke out against what he termed "December madness."

"People spend more than they can afford to spend for presents other people don't need or even like simply because they know their friends are doing the same thing. *I have to give you something just as nice as you give me.* Isn't that silly? If you ask me, the merchants ought to be ashamed of themselves for stirring people up the way they do. It's a disgrace."

When he talked like that, Mama tried to appear calm, even neutral. She loved giving presents, and she loved receiving them. She wondered what Papa would say if he knew that the presents for the Shakespeare Club members were under his bed on the sleeping porch. Both washtubs in the basement were filled with gifts, sheets draped over them for a camouflage. The Salvation Army presents were in the secret hiding place in the pantry and the ice pick that was needed to lift that section of wall was hidden where Papa couldn't find it even if he looked. All of us were up to our necks in plots and counterplots to keep Papa from knowing the extent of Mama's December madness.

Of course Mama knew that Papa's objections were deeper rooted than he let on. Their running argument as to how much Christmas we could celebrate in our house began in September or October, usually right after Yom Kippur. Papa didn't hesitate to place the blame for Mama's Christmas fixation on her family. "The only Jewish thing about the Levys is their name," he said.

"Christmas is for children, Max," Mama would say.

"Christmas is for Christian children," Papa would answer. "Jewish children have Hanukkah."

"But in this small town nobody celebrates Hanukkah but everybody celebrates Christmas. It's a time of love and good will, not just a religious festival. Our children know that other children hang up their stockings and believe in Santa Claus and exchange gifts and sing Christmas carols. To forbid ours from doing those things is downright cruel."

"Santa Claus and stockings aren't so bad," Papa admitted. "But those carols make me nervous."

I knew too well how nervous Papa got. When he and Mama came to the Glee Club's Christmas program I saw him in action. Papa attended everything his children performed in, the Christmas program included. I was a baritone and since the baritones stood on the front row of the Glee Club facing the audience I could sneak looks at Mama and Papa who were sitting on the front row of the school auditorium.

Papa was great during "Jingle Bells" and the "Winter Song" but when we started singing "Away in a Manger" and "Adeste Fidelis" he began to squirm. Our director Miss Sweet either had a fantastic sense of humor, or just didn't plain figure things out. She designated me as the soloist in "Silent Night." I was to—as she put it—"carry the lead" while the others hummed the melody behind me. All went well on the first chorus. Papa didn't object to the Holy Infant so tender and mild sleeping in heavenly peace. But the second time around, when I got to the words, "Christ the Saviour is born!" I saw Papa turn his head slightly and spit. I had to repeat the phrase and Papa did a repeat, too. I could tell from the way her eyes slanted almost to a close that Mama was going to strangle him if Papa spit one more time and I knew that no power on earth could stop him from doing so if he heard his own flesh and blood conclude a solo with the words of the forthcoming stanza, "Jesus, Lord, at Thy birth. Jesus, Lord, at Thy birth." It was an unorthodox thing for me to do but I did it. When I got to that point I didn't sing the words as they were written, but went back to the first verse instead and closed the song with "Sleep in heavenly peace, Sleep in heavenly peace." The members of the Glee Club humming away behind me thought that I had forgotten the words, but I knew exactly what I was doing. My voice wavered, but if I sounded a bit high at least I had the satisfaction of knowing that my father was dry.

With Mama insisting that we observe Christmas, and Papa insisting that we observe Hanukkah, something had to give. So we observed both. We had Santa Claus and the Hanukkah man, we had a Christmas tree and a Hanukkah bush, we had

Christmas decorations and Hanukkah lights. There were mutual concessions. Papa allowed us to say Merry Christmas to our friends and Mama joined us in wishing Happy Hanukkah to each other. Papa let us call the Hanukkah bush a Christmas tree in return for Mama's placing a star of David at the top of it. The arrangement suited us children because each of us received a gift on each of the eight nights of Hanukkah as well as several gifts on Christmas morning.

"Now my children know about their own heritage," Papa said.

Mama didn't comment then, but later I heard her say to Beulah, "The children get two Christmases for the price of one!"

Mama tried to have most of her Christmas gifts mailed out or delivered by the 22nd. That gave her time to do her Christmas cooking and baking, to get the children's presents organized, and to complete her Project Mrs. Santa Claus at the ranch.

Mama's most ambitious Christmas effort was directed at the tenant farmers. She found out the name of every child in every house that faced onto the dirt road which the county agent had facetiously designated Max Meyer's WPA Row and she used her own money to buy both useful and frivolous Christmas gifts for all of them. She remembered the parents, too, but the children got most of the presents. Ernie and Kate Cooper helped supply names, ages, needed items and a hiding place for the gifts in their own home.

Mama and I had our own spy system to determine when the coast was clear so we could take batches of gifts to the farm without Papa knowing about it. I never counted, but I must have driven her to the Coopers' house ten times with the presents we'd driven all over creation to buy. Mama needed three personal chauffeurs at Christmas.

The Coopers first started calling Mama Mrs. Santa Claus and the name stuck. Ernie and Kate would deliver Mama's gifts to each of the families the day before Christmas. Then early on Christmas Eve Papa (who knew nothing of the previous deliveries) drove to the ranch with his own annual "seasonal offering": pounds and pounds of candy, including candy canes of all sizes, apples, oranges, pears, and baskets of canned goods for the farmers' families. Since Ernie and Kate had never been told about the Hanukkah man they called Papa Santa Claus.

Mama's secrecy with her presents for the tenants was a private thing with her. It wasn't just the money part. She knew that if she told Papa about it he would have approved because he believed that money spent to make people happy was money well spent. It was the Christmas spirit within herself. She wanted to make Christmas an extraspecial occasion for each of the farmer families, yet she didn't want Papa to think she was trying to outdo him. "It's more fun when nobody knows," Mama said to me as we were driving home after depositing a load of presents at the Coopers. "Nobody knows the names of the wise men who brought gifts to the manger."

I'm sure no one will ever ask me to write "My Most Memorable Christmas" but if anybody does I've got the material. I've even got the theme song: "White Christmas," played on a kazoo.

Except it didn't happen on Christmas—it was Christmas Eve. And it wasn't just white—it was star-spangled . . . cockeyed . . . a veritable hell-on-wheels: with sleet, snow, freezing rain, ice, muck and chill thrown in.

Oklahomans dream of a white Christmas, same as everybody else, but they usually settle for a mild and green one. Not that year, the most memorable one. An arctic blizzard with all the trimmings blew in from the north at dusk on Christmas Eve, and within an hour the people and the landscape were frozen into a state of semiparalysis.

Supper was at six as usual. Mama brought a tray to the middle bedroom where I was in bed with a hawking, spitting, dripping, rasping cold. This was my first Christmas vacation from college and it was a miserable one.

"Just some soft boiled eggs, toast and tea," she said, examining my pajama tops to see if her flannel cloth saturated with goose grease was still pinned in place.

"To tell the truth, Mama, I'm not hungry. The castor oil—"

"That was three hours ago," she said. "You'll feel better when you eat. Feed a cold and starve a fever."

"That isn't what we learn in college," I said.

"Start eating," Mama said, "so I can eat dessert with Papa, Manny and Pearl. Go on. Start."

I didn't feel like it, but I started.

"It's my fault you caught cold," Mama said. "When you got home from college your resistance was low. I made you drive me every place and you got sick."

She looked outside for a long moment as though she were hypnotized by the snow and sleet, then frowned, and after making me swear I'd eat what was on the tray she went back to the dining porch where Papa was just finishing a bowl of blackberry cobbler made from blackberries she'd canned last summer. Pearl and Manny had already finished their supper so Mama sent them to my room to make sure I ate my eggs and toast.

"I don't think you'll have any trouble driving to the ranch,"

193

Mama said. When Papa didn't answer her, Mama looked at him nervously. "Do you?"

"I'm not going, Annie. Afraid to risk it."

"Max—"

"Look outside. It's still snowing."

"It's Christmas Eve, Max. I wouldn't insist but—it's *Christmas Eve.*"

"Weather's too bad. I put the car in the garage."

"Just five miles and it's paved highway." She looked at him closely. "You *bought* everything, didn't you?"

"You know I did. The whole back seat of the car is filled with stuff. I was going to take it this evening like I always do. But a person'd be crazy to go out in this."

"The children will be disappointed. They look forward to it."

"I'd ask Ernie to drive the pickup into town and get the treats but Kate would be mad. It's slick out there."

"Sonny is sick or he'd drive me," Mama said, half to herself.

"Look, Annie honey, I'd drive you if it were humanly possible. The farmers will understand."

"No, they won't."

"The goodies will taste just as good in a couple of days."

"Not to the kids. It's . . . *Christmas.*"

Mama said it so softly Papa couldn't guess her panic. She took Papa's cobbler dish, refilled it and gave him fresh coffee. All of which surprised him because Annie didn't give in so fast. "Thanks, honey dear," he said.

"Take your time," Mama said and sauntered slowly into the kitchen. Once there, she un-sauntered immediately and raced on the double for her closet. She put on two sweaters, a long knit muffler, dug out her old sealskin coat that was ripping at the seams, borrowed Pearl's wool-lined boots, my fur-lined gloves, and Manny's red stocking cap, took Papa's key ring out of his overcoat pocket, and marched out the front door.

Pearl, Manny and I saw Mama leave but it didn't occur to us she'd be going far. Probably to a neighbor's house to take something she'd baked for Christmas.

In a couple of minutes Papa ran into the room yelling, "Who's backing out the car?" He still had blackberry cobbler on his face.

We told Papa that Mama had gone outdoors.

"It can't be Mama," Manny said. "Mama can't drive."

By the time Papa had reached the front porch Mama already had the big car out of the driveway and into the street.

"She sure as hell is driving now!" Papa said, running back into the house for his coat. He figured he'd go after her in Pearl's Chrysler. "She's got my keys!" he screamed. "Damn it, Annie's taken my keys! She's out there driving the big LaSalle in a snowstorm! She doesn't know how to drive a LaSalle!"

"She doesn't know how to drive anything," Manny repeated.

"Goddamn it, Manny, shut up!"

"You shouldn't cuss like that, Papa," Pearl said. "It's Christmas Eve."

"I *know* it's Christmas Eve! That's why your crazy mother is driving a car she doesn't know how to drive and probably skidding off the road this very minute!" He looked at me. "What should we *do?*"

I started to say, "Pray" but thought better of it and said, "Call Ernie Cooper."

Papa called Ernie. He called him ten times in ten minutes.

"Look out for her, Ernie!" "Get a lantern so she'll find the driveway!" "Tell Kate to have something hot for her to drink!" "If she's not there in fifteen minutes I'm sending the Sapulpa Fire Department after her!"

On the eleventh call Kate answered. "She's here, Mr. Meyer. She and Ernie are already driving down the Row taking Christmas things inside each house. It's awful slippery but they're making it. Don't worry about her. She's having a real good time. It's stopped snowing here. Everything's white and pretty. Looks like Christmas ought to look! Should I call you when Mrs. Meyer starts for home?"

"Yes," Papa said wearily. Then, "No, maybe Ernie'll bring her." Then, "Call me when she starts for home."

Pearl lit the fire in the parlor and sat by the window looking for Mama. She kept a bath towel on her lap and wiped the pane with it when her breath steamed it up. Pretty soon we heard Pearl yell excitedly, "Here she comes! She's at the corner. I know it's Mama!"

"I thought Kate was going to—" Papa mumbled as he ran to the front door and then onto the front porch.

"Careful, Annie, careful," he yelled as Mama started to swing from the snowy street into the driveway. "Easy, sweetie . . . easyyyyyyyyyyyyy."

Whether it was the sight of Papa, bareheaded and in shirt sleeves, waving at her and shouting something she couldn't understand, or whether it was the sudden realization that she had done the impossible and was actually home alive, Mama misjudged the driveway, turned too soon, went over the curb and then continued to turn the wheel. The LaSalle skidded across our front yard, plowed a rut in the snow and mud and came to a stop with its radiator snuggled up to the big oak tree.

Before Mama could get out of the car Papa was in the yard embracing her and kissing her in a way none of us children had ever seen before. Pearl told me later that Papa was crying and when Mama saw him crying she began to cry, too.

By the time she had stamped the snow off her boots and come back to the bedroom to see me she was smiling happily.

"I hope your father doesn't catch cold," she said. "I wrapped my muffler around his neck and squeezed him into that warm fur coat of mine."

"What's he doing?"

"He's backing the car out of the front yard and putting it in the garage. I hope he puts the lights off. I don't know how." She looked at me propped up against my pillow and said, "Did the castor oil work?"

"*Mama!* I'm not a little boy any more. I'm in *college.*"

"Well, did it?"

"Yes."

"I thought so. You look better. Tell Pearl to give you and Manny some long stockings to hang on the mantel, then I want all you children in bed. It's Christmas Eve."

"And you're still Mrs. Santa Claus?"

She nodded and smiled. "I know how Santa Claus feels when it's all over. I'm tired."

"At least you proved you can drive. Anyone who can drive in that snow and ice can drive anywhere."

"Not me," Mama said, shaking her head. "I only did it because I had to. I can't drive because my wrists are weak. I've got weak wrists."

Argue with Mama.

197

8. Onward, Pilgrim Soldiers

Someone had to die or leave town before the Shakespeare Club could admit a new member. The founders wisely figured that what the club might lose in membership it would gain in prestige, so the size was irrevocably fixed at twelve. Sapulpa society was impressed with the club's exclusiveness but the men whose wives were charter members irreverently referred to the organization as the Dirty Dozen.

The climax of the local social season was the Shakespeare Club's annual Thanksgiving tea. Scheduled always for the day before Thanksgiving, this occasion was strictly members only, no guests allowed. The tea hours were from four in the afternoon until seven in the evening. This precipitated an annual grumble from the members' husbands who were forced to settle for late suppers, sometimes as much as an hour and a half later than usual, depending on when their wives finally got home.

Through the years efforts had been made to change the hours of the tea, but the motions were always voted down.

Mrs. Greenberg had so moved last year but Emily Smith had successfully opposed it. "Everything about our club is beautifully traditional," Mrs. Smith began. "If we change one thing we'll start changing others." And then she added in a burst of honesty, "I know how Mrs. Greenberg feels. Judge Smith is downright nasty when supper isn't ready and on the table at six sharp. But next time Mr. Greenberg complains about our Thanksgiving tea running late, quote the Bard. Ask him if he expects us to be like the merry wives of Windsor who had to 'wash, wring, brew, bake and scour' every blessed day! Tell him it won't hurt him to wait for his supper one day a year."

Emily Smith was launched and she had her Shakespearean clincher ready.

"Last year the judge started complaining before I had my hat off. He had the nerve to address me in a smarty voice: 'In the words of *Troilus and Cressida*, Have you not done talking yet?' I fixed him. I marched up to him, shook my finger under his nose and quoted Henry VIII, Act 5, Scene 3, line 99: 'I take my cause out of the gripes of men!'"

When it was Mama's turn to be hostess for the Thanksgiving tea she started a full week ahead of time baking cookies, pressing linens, polishing silver and shining crystal. The Shakespeare ladies had a way of seeing without looking. Mrs. Simpson, for instance, knew in a matter of moments exactly what Mama had acquired since the last time they had met at Mama's house.

"I know it's mean of me," Mama said to Beulah as they carefully washed the hand-painted plates that served as wall decorations on the high ledge that ran around the dining room, "but I can't wait to see Mrs. Simpson's face when she sees the new cut-glass lamp. She was the first to notice the flaw in the old one and felt it her duty to point it out to everybody present."

"Wait till she sees the cut-glass punch bowl," Beulah said. "She'll have a conniption fit."

"The weather's so warm I'm tempted to use the bowl and serve punch," Mama said. "I could float some sherbet in it." She shook her head. "Better not. We've always served tea and cookies at the Thanksgiving tea and I don't want to be the one to change it. I hope I've made enough cookies."

Mama always said that before a party. "I hope I've made enough." And of course she always made too many. This time there were four-o-clocks and fudge drops and thin chocolate cookies and fat chocolate cookies and date bars and orange crisps and black-and-whites and plain butter cookies and nut balls and fruit rings and heavenly little round chocolate balls filled with mocha cream. "My God, Annie," Papa said as Mama kept baking more and more, "are you expecting the Dir . . ." He caught himself before he said the Dirty Dozen. ". . . the Shakespeare Club . . . or some kind of army?"

"Oh, well," Mama said, "nothing will be wasted. The girls like to take one of each kind home with them for their families to taste." Seeing Papa now reminded her of the last time she'd entertained. He didn't put in an appearance until the last guest had gone. "I know that hen parties make you nervous, Max, but try to be here in time to say good-bye."

"I'll stay all afternoon and lecture on Shakespeare if you ask me to," Papa said, popping four cookies into his mouth one-two-three-four, then scooting out of the kitchen. Mama wished she were Emily Smith. Emily would have known the just-right Shakespearean barb to fling at him before he was out of sight.

Thanksgiving then was always the last Thursday of November. Even so, this year the weather was uncannily mild. There had been only two slight freezes so far and the days were sunny and warm. Afternoons warmed up to the upper sixties and low seventies and men actually went around in shirt sleeves.

When the Wednesday morning of the tea turned out to be still another sunshiny November anomaly Mama got a bright idea. I was eating breakfast when she asked, "Will you drive me to the ranch at noon?"

"Sure. Why?"

"Kate Cooper tells me the roses are still blooming in the nursery. I'll have a sandwich for you to eat while you drive and we can be out there and back before it's time for you to return to school."

Kate was right. As incredible as it was, the roses were blooming in the field rows the day before Thanksgiving. Mama and I cut five dozen extra-nice ones in less than half an hour. "Imagine," she kept saying, "roses in late November!" She placed them carefully in two large dishpans, sprinkled them with water she had brought with her, and we started home.

The vases were already lined up in a row on the table next to the kitchen sink and Mama started arranging the roses as soon as we brought them into the kitchen. "They'll be a sensation," Mama said, snipping stems and choosing colors for her arrangements. "For two cents I'd float some of these full red roses in the cut-glass punch bowl." She laughed. "Better not. Mrs. Simpson would have a stroke."

I was on my way out of the house, with a plate of cookies for my teacher in case I was tardy, when the telephone rang.

"Answer it, please," Mama said. "I've got my hands full of roses and Beulah is ironing."

"Hello," I said unenthusiastically.

"Hello, HELLO? Who's THIS?" The voice shouting at me sounded like . . . no, it couldn't be. Not at noon on long distance.

"This is Lewis."

"LULLY?"

I flinched. I hadn't been called Lully in years. I held the earpiece as far away as I could. My eardrum was still oscillating from the initial blast. "Hello, Uncle Julius."

"Let me talk to Annie."

"Come quick, Mama. It's Uncle Julius."

Drying her hands on her apron Mama said half to herself, "Hope something hasn't happened to Ed," as she ran from the kitchen to the telephone. "Julius?" she asked. Then, before he could answer. "What's wrong?"

"Nothing's WRONG!" Uncle Julius screamed. "Everything's RIGHT! I'm calling from Durant, Oklahoma. We're on our way to visit you."

Mama's knees lost their starch and she sank down to the edge of an ottoman.

Uncle Julius had grown impatient with the conversation and had handed the phone to Uncle Sam.

"Hello, Annie? I *say:* Annie? This is Sam. Have you got a big turkey for tomorrow? Have you got a really big turkey? Big enough for a celebration?"

"A twenty pounder, Sam . . . and everything to go with it. Is Mabel with you?"

"Mabel's here. And Julius. And me. And somebody *else*, Annie!" He was giggling. "Your new sister. I *say:* You've got a new *sister!*"

"Oh, for heaven's sake, Sam. Stop talking foolishness. Let me speak to Mabel."

"Mabel and Alice are in the bathroom. I'm not fooling you, Annie. Julius and Miss Alice got married yesterday. They invited Mabel and me to come along on their honeymoon. Mabel and I will sleep at your house. Julius and Alice will stay at a hotel. *Get* it? I *say*—"

"Oh, *Sam!*" Mama interrupted. Sam could be exasperating. "Julius and Alice *married?* After all these years! I'm happy for them." She started to explain that the Shakespeare Club would be there when they arrived but Sam kept babbling about inconsequentialities. She wanted to ask who was at the wedding, who performed the ceremony—a dozen other things, but all she could think to say was, "This is costing you money. Congratulate Miss Alice for me. Drive carefully. Good-bye."

I knew that if I didn't leave for school immediately I'd be late enough to be marked absent but I had to say something. "Uncle Julius called me Lully," I said accusingly.

"He was excited and just forgot," Mama reassured me. "I'll remind him you don't like it. Be nice to him. He just got married and he doesn't make sense. He married Miss Alice. . . . I simply mustn't call her *Miss* Alice any more. She's Alice now. . . . I didn't think they'd ever do it. Wait 'til Max hears the news that Julius Levy is *married!*" She started to get up, thought of Papa's reaction to a Baptist in the Levy family, and sank down again. "Sam's coming. And Mabel. It's a sort of family honeymoon."

"What about the party?"

"What about it?" she asked defensively. "There's plenty to eat . . . and if you mean the no-guests-allowed rule . . . why, you can't call my own family *guests*. If Mrs. Simpson so much as raises an eyebrow I'll tell her to her face that the members-only rule doesn't apply to an act of God . . . and *this* . . ." She pointed to the telephone. ". . . is an act of God!"

I could tell Mama was happy for Uncle Julius and Miss Alice and glad about the family honeymoon, but I also knew she was asking herself why it had to happen on this particular day.

"I'm late for school," I said. Then, impulsively, I added, "Cheer up, Mama. It could be worse."

"Worse?"

I said it and ran. "They could be bringing Ossie Honeycocker with them!"

For some obscure reason that no one remembered, the tradition-trapped Shakespeare Club had started the custom of its members wearing Pilgrim costumes at their Thanksgiving tea. Not Pilgrim women—Pilgrim men! With the possible exception of Mrs. Abernathy who was a marvelous seamstress and had designed herself a handsome silk coat-and-trousers outfit, every member of the club hated the Pilgrim bit and would gladly have voted to change the rule. But no one dared take the initiative so the members let out already-let-out seams, turned under frayed cuffs, lined and relined threadbare pant bottoms and tried to get through one more Thanksgiving in borderline-shabby clothes the original Pilgrims would have contributed to a missionary barrel.

The upper parts of the costumes weren't so bad. Some even had a modicum of flair to them. The freshly washed blouses atoned for the tired brown coats with their cardboard-extension coattails.

It was from the waist down that trouble set in. Most of

the lower garments consisted of shiny, easily wrinkled cambric trousers that stuck to the behind with the slightest dampness. There was a uniform bulge around each Pilgrim's calf where the pant leg had been stuffed into a long black or brown ribbed stocking. The shoes were mostly black patent leather oxfords with silver belt buckles stolen from their husbands and sewn on by hand.

One or two of the members had free-lanced the bottoms. Mrs. Anderson had dyed a pair of sateen bloomers brown and had worn these for the last five years. Mrs. Greenberg, whose ample endowments had split too many conventional pantaloons, finally settled for a pair of her son's dark brown knickers.

The stovepipe hats would have given an honest-to-goodness Pilgrim nightmares. Most of the original stovepipes, covered with brown cloth, which was also tucked around and under the cardboard brims, had been bashed in from years of storage on closet shelves but they were still being worn. Mrs. Longmire had reluctantly decided to give up her stovepipe in favor of a brown straw sailor which looked even more bizarre than a dented stovepipe on this last Thursday of November. "I'm glad she cut the streamers off," Mrs. Abernathy said the first time Mrs. Longmire appeared in it.

Mama still wore a brown sateen hat, blocked around a two-foot tall cardboard filler. It was hers now, but the head-covering had originally belonged to me. I had worn it for my first stage appearance in a second-grade class play. (It would be more accurate to call it "a play given by our second-grade class" because the play itself was below second class in quality.) My part had consisted of one line. I ran onto the stage, shouted, "The Indians are coming!" and ran off again. Mama felt self-righteous in wearing the hat at the

Thanksgiving teas through the years because, as she put it, "What a waste to make a hat just for a four-word announcement."

"You look pretty, Miz Meyer," Beulah said when Mama walked into the kitchen in her costume. "That hat gives you height." Then she added soothingly, "Don't you worry about a single thing. Everything's gonna be all right."

"Thanks, Beulah, but I think I look awful. And I keep wanting to yell, 'The Indians are coming!' every time I look in a mirror. Thank goodness, it's only once a year we have to dress like this and nobody sees us but ourselves."

Mama hadn't worked up the courage to tell Beulah that four hungry guests from Texas were driving toward 215 South Oak Street that very moment. One thing at a time was all Beulah could absorb and twelve Pilgrims for tea was enough for now. Mama said a private word of thanksgiving that the tea would be almost over by the time the Levys arrived.

Precisely at four, Mama peeked through the parlor curtains and saw Mrs. Smith and Mrs. Croston mincing down the sidewalk in their Pilgrim costumes. If the weather had been the least bit snappish the club members might have hidden their getups under coats or sweaters (Mrs. Abernathy always affected a brown herringbone tweed cape), but most of the Pilgrims walked into this Indian summer's day unarmed and unadorned. From this first glimpse, Mama made a mental note to keep the Texas visitors occupied while the guests were leaving. If the Shakespeareans looked this outlandish from the front, only God knew what a rear view would disclose.

Mama welcomed the Shakespearean Pilgrims, offered to take their wraps (Mrs. Abernathy, perspiring noticeably under her heavy cape, was the only one who came wrapped), and made them comfortable in the parlor. For once, Mama was glad that Papa built everything big. Even with its baby grand piano, the parlor was large enough to accommodate twice this many people without anybody having to spill over into the adjoining dining room.

There was a barely discernible abstractness about Mama. It went deeper than the normal preparty flutterings of a conscientious hostess. Beulah must have sensed it with her, *"Don't you worry. . . . Everything is gonna be all right."* Everything *should* be all right. The house was cleaned to an inch of its life, the tea table in the dining room set to perfection, the refreshments in the kitchen waiting patiently under tea towels to be sampled and praised, but there was something she couldn't put her finger on. Not something bad. She didn't feel it was *bad.* Something—*different.* No, it couldn't be Sam. Julius simply wouldn't let Sam drink on the trip. Mabel? Mabel was all right. Her uncertainties and vacillations were mainly confined to the second floor of the Levy home. Put Mabel in a social gathering and she was a credit to the family. Miss Alice? She'd be fine. *I'll kiss her first, ahead of the others, and call her Alice and everything will be all right there.* Still . . . The prickly, unsettled feeling persisted so strongly that when Mama caught Mrs. Simpson with her nose in the base of the cut-glass lamp looking for the flaw that wasn't there she was too preoccupied to be triumphant.

When Mrs. Longmire ended her opening prayer with the words "In Jesus's name," it was only natural that Mama would think of Papa. He'd promised to appear shortly before seven but to be on the safe side she had called Ernie Cooper earlier and made Ernie promise to get Papa started for home around six-thirty. Mama went down her mental check list.

Pearl was helping Beulah in the kitchen. The boys were home from school and playing outdoors. Everything was in order. But . . ."

After the opening prayer Mrs. Jennings read the 107th Psalm ("O give thanks unto the Lord, for He is good") after explaining that the Pilgrims prayed those same words together before sitting down to their first Thanksgiving feast.

The rest of the program was in the nature of a well-worn blueprint. Mrs. Greenberg gave her yearly paper entitled "Shakespeare and the Pilgrims," which she had now embroidered to the point where Shakespeare's "recently departed spirit" was in the hold of the *Mayflower* planting noble thoughts in the minds of the Pilgrims on the deck above. (What his spirit had been doing for the four years from his death in 1616 to the Mayflower departure in 1620 Mrs. Greenberg didn't say.) She ended her talk each year with the same inspiring words: "Shakespeare died that the Pilgrims might live!"

Before the applause died down Mrs. Greenberg excused herself to enact her own traditional Thanksgiving tea rite. She went to the bathroom, took off her corset, hid it in the linen closet under the bath towels, then returned to the meeting. She would drive by early on Thanksgiving morning, as she always did, to pick it up.

> "I hate ingratitude more in a man
> Than lying, vainness, babbling drunkenness . . ."

That would be Emily Smith on "Shakespearean Gratitude and Ingratitude," Mama thought, only half listening. She found it difficult to focus on what was being said on the program. She was more interested in looking out the window that faced the driveway, expecting to see a car driven by a small man with a large voice. She kept losing the thread of what Mrs. Smith was saying as her eyes searched the street for Texas pilgrims, due to land at any moment.

Sure enough, just as Mrs. Smith was declaiming with feeling

"Or any ill escaped, or good attained,
Let us remember still,
Heaven chalked the way that brought us thither!"

there was a sustained honking that started at the corner and grew louder and louder until the Levy car was parked on the driveway. Uncle Julius was leaning on the horn and Aunt Mabel, holding her hands over her ears, was obviously yelling, "Stop that noise, Julius! Julius Levy, take your hand off that horn *this minute!*"

Mrs. Smith, who was almost finished anyway, bowed abruptly and sat down.

Mama rushed outside to welcome them, kissed her new sister-in-law and hugged her brother Julius, then kissed Mabel and Sam in that order.

The visitors couldn't help noticing Mama's strange clothes. Sam said it first. "For God's sake, Annie. I *say*: For God's sake, what have you got *on?* Have you lost your mind?"

Mama laughed. "It's club day. I'm supposed to be a Pilgrim." She decided to omit the Shakespeare part. "And you're just in time for refreshments!"

Mama was proficient at introductions. She even stressed the "*Mrs.* Julius Levy" in a way to please the newlyweds.

Mabel, who had protested all the way into the house that she looked too tacky to mingle with Mama's friends in their dressy clothes, relaxed when she saw the Shakespeareans. By no standard known to womankind could the tea be called "dressy." Mabel found it hard to stop staring at Mrs. Greenberg's knickers.

As for Sam, he couldn't believe his eyes. All these women in their crazy costumes! If he wasn't positive he was in Sapulpa, Oklahoma, he'd swear he was in one of the women's wards of the asylum at the wrong end of Levy Avenue.

Uncle Sam wandered into the kitchen and found me systematically sampling each kind of cookie to be served at the tea. "Hello, Harry Lewis," he said.

I think I would have kissed him if my mouth hadn't been full of fudge drops. Even though high school boys didn't kiss grown men I still think I would have kissed him because I dearly loved Uncle Sam.

"Here," he said, pressing a five-dollar bill into my hand. "There's bound to be a bottle of whiskey around here someplace. Find it for me."

"There's the castor oil whiskey," I said, trying to be helpful.

When Uncle Sam looked surprised I explained, "Mama pours a little of it into castor oil when we have to take it."

"I *say*: Forget the castor oil and produce the whiskey."

I did as I was told.

It was working out better than Mama dared hope it would. All of the members, including Mrs. Simpson, took it for granted that Mama's relatives had surprised her and, good Pilgrims that they were, made a special effort to make the visitors feel welcome. Mrs. Smith gave a Shakespearean toast to the bride, holding high her cup of tea and proclaiming:

"The chief perfections of that lovely dame—
Had I sufficient skill to utter them—
Would make a volume of enticing lines. . . ."

As the other members chimed in with "Hear! Hear!" Miss Alice blushed nicely and Uncle Julius covered his embarrassment by lighting a cigar. Even though it was the same stinking brand he always smoked, the club ladies didn't seem to mind a bit.

"You've *made* the party!" Mama whispered to Mabel. "It's the most successful Thanksgiving tea we've ever had!"

The more people talked, the higher the spirits. The higher the spirits, the more people ate.

"Annie's cookies are vanishing like snow on a warm day," Aunt Mabel said.

"Plenty more where these came from," Beulah said, trading an empty platter for a full one.

The confusion resulting from the serving of refreshments, the laughter and toasts and Uncle Julius's stentorian sallies kept the noise level so high that the sound of the approaching army was muffled until it was almost upon them.

It was an army, all right: the Salvation Army, and it was parading in the opposite direction from its usual line of march up Dewey Avenue to Main Street. On this singular day it tooted and blared its way from the Hut to an unaccustomed target on Oak Street.

The townspeople in their homes were stunned at the unexpected sound of "Onward, Christian Soldiers" in the residential section and ran to their front doors to look out. Excited children who had just finished supper begged to go outside as far as the sidewalk to wave at the marchers and because the day was still warm their bewildered parents let them do it.

Only a person familiar with the Army's regular formations could have detected a change of lineup, but on this day Mrs. Major Miller, who was usually last in line in case a spectator wished to buy a copy of *War Cry*, marched side by side with Major Miller at the head of the procession. Instead of *War Crys* she clutched in her right hand a small box which she held extended, keeping time with it to the boom-boom-boom of Old Fats's drum.

Pearl heard them first. "Listen," she said, outshouting Uncle Julius. *"Listen!"*

The drumbeats were louder now and Captain Bledsoe's cornet began to punctuate the syllables: "ON-ward, CHRIS-tian sooooold-IERS, MARCH-ing as to WARRRRRR. . . ."

The guests became suddenly quiet. Mama, who was sitting on the hard piano bench, was the first to sense a relationship of the Army to her tea. As the little band entered our drive-way and aimed for the front porch Mama sat up straighter on the bench, held her head high, kept her eyes on the front door and braced herself for whatever was to come.

Armies don't knock, and this one was no exception. Major Miller turned the handle and the door opened. Without missing a beat he led the parade into the house: first, he and Mrs. Miller, then Old Fats, pounding the smudged skin of his battle-scarred drum, then Steve (whose trombone almost but not quite caught Mrs. Simpson from behind as she turned to move her chair to make more room for the visitors), then Teresa, Captain Bledsoe, Billy Bledsoe who was now a private in the Army and Corporal Mary Wade. Each time Corporal Wade struck her cymbals the glass tear drops on the cut-glass lamp shivered. It was hard to tell who was the more surprised: the Shakespeareans and Levys at being invaded by a singing Army . . . or the Salvation Army itself at finding a houseful of facsimile Pilgrims at an hour when they expected to find only the family group.

They formed a semicircle around the piano, addressing themselves to Mama who was perched like a bird on the edge of the spindly-legged bench. The Army, used to in-attentive and even hostile audiences, seemed oblivious to the other people in the room.

As Major Miller cleared his throat to speak, Mama saw the lights of Papa's car. *Right on schedule,* she thought. Then, *Damn it. Right on schedule.* And then, *I hope he goes to the back door.* She tried through intensive concentration to plant the idea in his mind. . . . *Back door, Max . . . Go to the back door. . . . Back door . . .*

"Sister Annie," the Major began, in much the same voice that he used to heal sinners. "We come to honor you in the name of our Lord, Jesus Christ!"

Mama glanced quickly at Julius and Mabel, neither of whom had moved a muscle at the words. Mama's head tilted a degree higher with pride at being a Levy.

"You have worked with all your heart in the spirit of the Master to help the poor and befriend the needy! Therefore . . . the Salvation Army does hereby proclaim you, Sister Annie Meyer, Citizen of the Year!"

To her everlasting credit, Emily Smith started the round of applause which served as a release for the concentrated emotional tension in the room. She obviously had a Shake-spearean amen on the tip of her memory but Major Miller continued his speech before she could get it out.

"Here is your medal of honor for being a soldier of God!" the Major said, taking the medallion from the small velvet-lined box his wife had been holding. He pinned the medal neatly on Mama's brown cambric coatlet.

Major Miller smiled, stepped back, and at the precise instant that Papa walked in through the front door Major Miller pointed to Mama and said, "Sister Annie, you are the perfect example of a good Christian woman!"

Papa spat.

"Thank you, friends," Mama said hurriedly. "You must have some tea and cookies and meet everybody."

"After the hymn," the Major said. He gave Mama a kindly look. "Want to guess which one?"

Mama knew which one.

"Friends, some know it as 'O Boundless Salvation.' We call it 'Sister Annie's favorite!'"

Captain Bledsoe blew the first note for pitch and the Millers, Fats, Teresa and Corporal Wade began to sing,

"O boundless salvation! Deep ocean of love . . ."

Papa, bewildered at what he had just seen and heard, retreated to the kitchen where he was even more bewildered to find Sam Levy. Sam, who was feeling pretty good from the whiskey, gave Papa an unusually cordial hello.

Papa turned to me. "You're pale, Sonny Boy. What's going on here?"

"Nothing's going on here," I said. "It's all happening in the parlor. The Shakespeare Club has eaten twelve dozen cookies, the Salvation Army's giving Mama a medal and Uncle Julius and Miss Alice are man and wife."

"My God!" was Papa's succinct response to all of it.

If I looked pale to Papa there was a reason for it. Uncle Sam, who had sneaked a look at the Army people, was fervently attempting to bribe me into bringing the beautiful Teresa to the back bedroom to meet him. "Tell her to bring her tambourine. I want to put some money on it for the good of—I *say:* for the good of the cause." His two-dollar starter had grown to five and then to ten when Papa arrived in the nick of time to save the day for me and spoil everything for Uncle Sam.

I left Uncle Sam with Papa and got to the parlor in time for the last part of the song.

> "And now, Hallelujah! The rest of my days
> Shall gladly be spent in promoting His praise. . . ."

The guests were standing, all of them: the Shakespeare Club, Uncle Julius, Miss Alice, Aunt Mabel—everybody in the crowded room was standing except Mama who was still on the piano bench looking up at the Salvation Army people playing and singing to her. I shall always remember her face, the expression on it. As though she never wanted this moment to end. Being part of it all gave me goosebumps. I felt what others were feeling—a warmth and oneness that traveled through each of us in that circle of love that began with the Salvation Army and ended with Mama.

The hymn was almost finished now and everybody joined in:

> "Who opened His bosom to pour out this sea
> Of boundless salvation for you and for me."